支持项目：哈尔滨工程大学研究生公共课教改立项
"整合优化教学资源，创建研究生公共英语课程国际化人才培养模式"

学术交流英语

主　编　陈海霞
副主编　周薇薇　梁　红
　　　　孙淑娟　张鹏蓉
主　审　邓晓明

哈尔滨工业大学出版社

内 容 简 介

本书以参加国际学术会议和论文撰写为主线,对国际会议准备阶段和进行过程中的信函往来、学术论文的撰写、论文的宣读、会议中的学术交流等进行了较为完整的讲述。全书共分为五个单元,每个单元设立一个主题。

本书主要适于高等院校研究生的教学使用,同时也可供具备一定英语基础的各学科领域的学者参考使用。本书旨在帮助大家提高学术英语的表达能力,克服参加国际学术交流中的语言障碍。

图书在版编目(CIP)数据

学术交流英语/陈海霞主编. — 哈尔滨:哈尔滨工业大学出版社,2019.7
ISBN 978-7-5603-8396-5

Ⅰ.①学… Ⅱ.①陈… Ⅲ.①学术交流-英语-研究生-教材 Ⅳ.①G321.5

中国版本图书馆 CIP 数据核字(2019)第 131977 号

策划编辑	王桂芝
责任编辑	王桂芝 张 荣
出　　版	哈尔滨工业大学出版社
社　　址	哈尔滨市南岗区复华四道街 10 号 邮编 150006
传　　真	0451-86414749
网　　址	http://hitpress.hit.edu.cn
印　　刷	黑龙江艺德印刷有限责任公司
开　　本	710mm×1000mm 1/16 印张 14 字数 300 千字
版　　次	2019 年 7 月第 1 版　2019 年 7 月第 1 次印刷
书　　号	ISBN 978-7-5603-8396-5
定　　价	34.00 元

(如因印装质量问题影响阅读,我社负责调换)

前言 Preface

随着我国研究生培养水平的提高和科研工作的蓬勃发展，较多的研究生和青年学者撰写论文，参与国际学术交流，与国际同领域的专家、学者进行互动与切磋。其中，研究生的英语科技论文撰写水平、参与国际交流的英语表达能力将起到至关重要的作用。所以，开设相关的课程，在教学中贯穿"国际化、学术化"的思路逐渐成为高等院校研究生英语培养的趋势。

本书结合教学实践和研究生的培养目标，以满足目前学生的需求、培养学生跨文化交际的意识、提高学生英语学术写作能力和国际学术交流能力为目标，在原有《学术英语教程》的基础上，对原书进行了缩减和修改，增加了教师课堂教学的实用内容，减少了理论讲述部分，补充了最新的范例。

全书共分五个单元。

第一单元全面介绍参加国际学术会议的准备工作，包括对国际学术会议的总体介绍、会议通知、会议征稿、会议日程的举例和讲解。

第二单元按照参加国际学术会议的步骤，对国际学术会议之前可能发生的信件往来进行介绍，包括会议邀请函、会议接收函和会议拒绝函。

第三单元开始讲解学术写作部分。以部分学术论文为例，对学术论文的各个组成部分、包括的内容、写作要点等进行介绍。本章的重点是介绍英语学术论文的题目、摘要、正文、参考文献和附录的撰写。

第四单元介绍与国际学术会议相关的各种过程、发言的注意事项，以及如何准备相关的发言稿，其中包括会议主持、会议发言、会议提问及回答要点等。

第五单元介绍在国际学术交流过程中涉及的一些实用文本的写作，包括申请信写作、履历的写作、个人自述的写作，以及介绍如何参加面试。

本书依据实践需求，以任务式教学法为主导，按照参加国际学术会议的程序将讲解的内容分成不同的板块，教师可根据板块内容设定与主题相关的实践任务，包括写作、课上练习、课下准备、会议发言模拟、会议主持模拟等环节，使学生学到的书本知识能够通过实践加以印证。

本书重实践、重例证，在书中提供了大量的实例，以便学生巩固学到的知识，学以致用。

本书在编写过程中参考了国内外部分相关书籍和网站上的相关资料，在此，向提供材料的作者表示诚挚的谢意。同时感谢邓晓明老师和哈尔滨工业大学出版社在本书的出版过程中给予的帮助和支持。

《学术交流英语》的编写是我们在课程改革上的一种尝试和推进，在编写过程中出现的不妥和疏漏之处敬请专家和读者批评指正。

作　者

2019 年 5 月

目录
Content

Unit 1 Preparations for International Conference ········· 1
  Task 1: Introduction ········· 2
  Task 2: Conference Notice ········· 7
  Task 3: Call for Conference Papers ········· 12
  Task 4: Conference Agenda/Programs ········· 20

Unit 2 International Letter Exchange ········· 23
  Task 1: Business Letters ········· 24
  Task 2: Letters of Invitation ········· 34
  Task 3: Letters of Reply ········· 40

Unit 3 Academic Paper Writing ········· 45
  Task 1: General Knowledge of Academic Papers ········· 46
  Task 2: Title ········· 54
  Task 3: Abstract ········· 59
  Task 4: Body of an Academic Paper ········· 69
  Task 5: Acknowledgements, References, Notes ········· 122
  Task 6: Avoid Errors in Academic Writing ········· 133

Unit 4 International Conference ········· 141
  Task 1: Chairing a Meeting ········· 142
  Task 2: Making a Presentation ········· 152
  Task 3: Asking and Answering Questions ········· 172

Unit 5   Practical Writing ······ 182
Task 1: Letters of Application ······ 183
Task 2: Cover Letters ······ 191
Task 3: Curriculum Vitae(CV) ······ 197
Task 4: Personal Statement ······ 208

Unit 1

Preparations for International Conference

Learning Objectives

In this unit, you will learn to accomplish the following tasks:

➢ Task 1: To know introduction of international academic conference
➢ Task 2: To get information from Conference Notice
➢ Task 3: To familiarize Call for Conference Papers
➢ Task 4: To get information from Conference Program

Task 1: Introduction

This part is an introduction to International Academic Conferences. You will learn:
- ◆ Introduction of various international meetings
- ◆ Principal activities in an international conference
- ◆ How to prepare for the conference

⧗ General Knowledge

As an academic researcher in any field, you must feel increasingly required to participate in international conferences, which is a way of broadening your exposure to academic circles and becoming actively involved in scholarly activities in the world. You may have chances to attend various meetings, narrow or broad in scope, such as conferences, symposium, congresses, conventions, colloquia, forums, summits, seminars, workshops, round tables, special panels, poster sessions, exhibits, or other similar situations. Your success in attending a meeting is based on how effective you are. This unit is designed to help you understand the important steps for preparing for attending a meeting and give you a variety of knowledge and techniques for performing effectively. With the necessary knowledge, practical skills and useful suggestions provided in this unit, you can make a difference and make yourself successful in attending international meetings.

1. Types

There are different kinds of international meetings and they have different names such as conference, congress, convention, forum, seminar, symposium, workshop, etc(Tab. 1.1).

Unit 1 Preparations for International Conference

Tab. 1.1 Different Types of International Meetings

Names	Chinese names	Introduction
Meetings	会议的总称	Meeting is a general term and it can mean any kind of gathering for a particular purpose.
Conference	大型专业会议	Conference is a formal and large-scale meeting which is organized on a particular subject to bring together people who have common interests.
Convention	年会	Convention is a formal and routine meeting of members, representatives, or delegates, as of a political party, fraternal society, profession, or industry.
Congress	代表大会	Congress is usually a large-scale formal assembly of representatives, as of various nations, to discuss issues, ideas, and policies of public interest.
Forum	论坛	Forum is a public meeting or presentation involving a discussion usually among experts and often including audience participation.
Seminar	专题研讨会	Seminar is a class-like meeting, where participants discuss a particular topic or subject that is presented by several major speakers. The scale of a symposium is usually smaller than that of a conference.
Symposium	专题讨论会	Symposium is a meeting at which experts, scholars, and other participants of a particular field discuss a particular subject. A symposium is usually narrower and more specific in the range of topics than a conference.
Workshop	讲习研讨班	Workshop is a discussion and demonstration of practical work on a particular subject when a group of people learn about the subject by sharing their knowledge or experience.

2. Organizing institutions of an academic conference

Conferences are usually organized either by a scientific society or by a group of researchers with a common interest. Larger meetings may be handled on behalf of the scientific society by a Professional Conference Organizer.

- Organizing Committee
- Scientific Program Committee/Academic Committee
- Advisory Committee
- Local Organizing Committee
- Secretariat
- Contact Person

3. Principal conference activities:

Different kinds of activities may be involved in an international conference such as formal meetings, informal meetings, audio and visual presentations, visits, etc.

(1) Formal meetings.

Formal meetings usually include general assembly, plenary session, parallel session (panel session), poster session, etc.

- General assembly:

A general assembly is usually attended by all the participants of the conference and sometimes by government officials and reporters. A general assembly is characterized by the opening ceremony, welcome speeches, general speeches, and the closing ceremony.

- Plenary session (keynote session):

It usually refers to a session in a conference which is open to all (or a large number) of attendant speakers, who may each contribute prepared material. In the plenary session of an international academic conference, keynote speeches relevant to the theme of the conference will be given by well-known experts. Keynote speeches will take longer time than ordinary paper presentations which take place in a parallel session.

- Panel session (parallel session):

A panel session is a small-scale meeting and several parallel sessions are usually held simultaneously. Such a session is for participants to present their papers and usually, a special topic is arranged for a particular parallel session.

- Poster session:

A poster session is an occasion on which papers are posted on boards or walls in a specially separated area of the meeting place. The participants can go to read the posted papers and discuss them with the author if he/she is there.

(2) Informal meetings.

Informal meetings refer to informal communication among participants of the conference. Informal meetings may take the form of "free information exchange", "free paper presentation", "free communication", etc.

(3) Audio and visual presentations.

On some occasions, professional presentations need audio or visual aids. Such audio or visual aids may be the use of slide projectors, videotapes, short film projectors, PowerPoint, etc.

(4) Visits and other social activities.

At a conference, there can also be visits and other social activities in or around the host city, such as visits to historical or scenic spots, visits to famous research institutes, universities, or museums, banquets, various parties, concerts, games, etc. These activities are held to provide the participants with more opportunities to come into contact with each other and establish friendship.

4. The process of a conference

Receiving a conference notice call for conference papers
↓
Submitting a paper abstract
↓
Receiving notice of acceptance
↓
Submitting the full paper
↓
Receiving the invitation to the conference
↓
Getting to know the program of the conference
↓
Attending the international conference
↓
Presenting in the conference

Related Words:

summit　峰会，首脑会议
round-table　圆桌会议
special panel　专题讨论会
general assembly　全体会议
plenary session　主题发言会
panel session　分组会议
poster session　墙报专场，展示会议
question & answer session　问答会
coffee/tea break　茶歇
welcoming reception/banquet　欢迎酒会
buffet　自助餐
registration　报到
invited speaker　特邀发言人
keynote speaker　主题发言人
keynote speech　主题发言
paper presentation　论文宣读
honorary chairman　名誉主席
executive secretary　执行秘书
sponsor　主办方
organizer　承办方
secretariat　秘书处
platform　主席台
organizing committee　组委会
academic committee　学术委员会

Unit 1 Preparations for International Conference

Task 2: Conference Notice

⌛ General Knowledge

A conference notice is a good way for the prospective participants to acquire general information about the conference. Though a conference notice is not supposed to be very long, it should give all the needed information as much as possible. A conference notice usually includes the name of the conference, the date and the place, the organizer, the purpose, the key topics, prospective participants, ways to register, registration fees, the conference agenda, the contact channels and so on.

⌛ Format and Content of a Conference Notice

- Title of the conference
- Dates and location of the conference
- Conference description/objectives
- Theme of the conference
- Background information
- Agenda
- Registration and cost
- Related information
- Participants
- Sponsoring agency
- Organizing party
- Contact

⌛ Sample Demonstration

Environment-Behavior Research Association
11th International Symposium on Environment-Behavior Research
EBRA2019

Guangzhou, China

- Theme

Ecological and Wisdom: Towards a Healthy Urban and Rural Environment

The process of China's reform and opening up is a magnificently rapid urbanization process. During this time, Chinese urban and rural areas are experiencing industrialization, marketization, globalization and information time's change, then the living environment and living standards of these areas are rising at the same time, and some significant challenges are also facing, like the shortage of resources, environmental pollution, etc. Meanwhile, the living environment, the mode of production and the lifestyle of peoples have been changing; they have to face with a series of environmental psychological problems like the environment crowded, the environment adaptation, the environment pressure, the living circle reconstruction and so on. Facing the times change in the globalization context, in order to achieve the ideal for the ecological, wisdom and healthy urban and rural environment, we warmly welcome and sincerely hope that the man of insight attended the symposium from around the world, who can offer advice and suggestions, to discuss the environmental behavior issues together under the contemporary social development changes.

- Organizers

Environment-Behavior Research Association (EBRA)

South China University of Technology (SCUT)

- Co-organizations

State Key Laboratory of Subtropical Building Science, SCUT

- Date

7-9 November, 2019

- Venue

School of Architecture, South China University of Technology, Guangzhou, China

- Invitation

MERA (Man-Environment Research Association), JAPAN

IAPS (International Association for People-Environment Studies), EUROPE

EDRA (Environmental Design Research Association), U.S.A.

HERS (Human-Environment Relations Studies), TAIWAN

- Theme

Ecological and Wisdom: Towards a Healthy Urban and Rural Environment

- Topics

01-Theories and Methodology of Environment-Behavior Research

02-Environment-Behavior Education and Practice

03-Spatial Perception and Cognition

04-Ecological and Sustainable Environment and Lifestyle of Urban and Rural Areas

05-Environment and Lifestyle Change in Rapid Urbanization

06-Wisdom city, Healthy Community and Residential Building

07-Research and Practice of Post Occupancy Evaluation (POE)

08-Climate Change, Disasters and Environmental Safety Design

09-Protection of Cultural Heritage and Environment-Behavior

10-Environment-Behavior of Special Population Groups of the Aged, Children and so on

11-Quality of Green Public Buildings and Public Spaces

12-Research of Environment-Behavior and Digitization

- Programs

Keynote Speeches

Keynote speeches will be delivered by several renowned scholars from the West, Asia and China. Please pay attention to the notifications on EBRA website.

Oral Sessions

The authors of accepted oral papers will be invited to the symposium. (The accepted papers will be formally published on the symposium proceedings by South China University of Technology Press.)

Posters

The authors of accepted posters will be invited to the symposium. (The accepted posters will be formally published on the symposium proceedings by South China University of Technology Press.)

Symposia

According to the submitted papers, symposia on the hot research topics of environment-behavior will be organized. Please pay attention to the notifications on EBRA website.

Café con

This is informal forum, during the café time, you will encounter …

- Language

English and Chinese

- Call for Papers

The symposium is calling for abstracts of papers addressing environment-behavior research in general and symposium themes in particular. Authors of accepted abstracts will be notified and invited to submit full papers. An international referee panel will be formed to review all the full papers. Accepted full papers will be published in the symposium proceedings by the South China University of Technology Press (notice: at least one of the authors should register and attend the symposium.

- Paper Abstracts

The Requirements of Abstract: Words in 500 words or so. Standard format of the text will be Times Roman 12, 1.5 spaced. Please observe the following requirements:

(1) Author's name(s) and affiliation.

(2) Title.

(3) Text of 500 words including references.

(4) 3-5 keywords.

The entire submission (1~4) should be less than 500 words.

Full paper requirements please refer to EBRA website later.

After the submission of abstracts, the authors will be required to provide each copy of the full papers in English and Chinese, and an A4 size page of the outline in English.

- Important Dates

15 March, 2019   Abstract submission deadline;

25 March, 2019   Notification of abstract acceptance, Invitations to the authors;
30 May, 2019   Full paper submission deadline;
20 July, 2019   Notification of full paper acceptance;
20 August, 2019   Start of pre-registration and revised paper submission deadline;
25 September, 2019   Pre-registration deadline;
6 November, 2019   Symposium registration;
7-9 November, 2019   Symposium date.

Homepage: http://www.ebra.cn
Email: 9ebra2019@163.com
Secretary: Jiang Mengting +86-186-64644636 EBRA14 Organizing Committee
   10 January, 2019

⌛ Check Your Understanding

Answer the following questions according to what you have been informed.

(1) Who are the sponsors of the conference?
(2) How long will the conference last and what is the agenda?
(3) What is the conference held for?
(4) If one wants to participate in the conference, how can he register?

Task 3: Call for Conference Papers

General Knowledge

Call for papers includes more detailed information about the conference scope (theme), conference areas (topics of interest), and other activities held during the conference. The meeting committees will work out a general program, including a call for papers, which is to notify the prospective participants of the conference.

The call for papers must be written in order to notify the prospective participants of the conference. It usually involves information concerning the conference theme, date(s), venue, objectives, topics of interests, plenary (keynote) speakers, sponsors, Organizing Committee, the requirement for paper submission (abstract submission deadline, acceptance notification, full paper submission), registration fee, and contact information. When the events begin to take place, details are discussed, such as nametags, proper signs, the program, the sound system, the lighting, food, and the arrangement for someone to answer queries.

Format of Call for Conference Papers

- Title, date, venue, theme, background, objectives
- Topics to be discussed
- Keynote speakers
- Papers and submission
- Registration fee
- Organizing institution and committee, sponsors
- Other activities
- Contact information

Sample Demonstration

SIBR-Thammasat 2019 BANGKOK CONFERENCE ON
INTERDISCIPLINARY BUSINESS & ECONOMICS RESEARCH
June 9th-10th, 2019, Bangkok

CALL FOR PAPER

The SIBR 2019 Bangkok Conference on Interdisciplinary Business & Economics Research will be held on June 9th (Sunday) and 10th (Monday), 2019 at the Emerald Hotel in Bangkok, Thailand. The conference theme is "The Interdisciplinary Approach to Research, Innovation and Practice". The SIBR conference brings together academics and professionals from all business and economics disciplines to share latest research findings and brainstorm new research ideas across disciplines. It is a unique forum for researchers with cross-disciplinary interests to meet and interact. Research papers using theoretical, quantitative, qualitative, or mixed-methods approaches are encouraged as are those using interdisciplinary approaches.

ORGANIZERS
Society of Interdisciplinary Business Research (SIBR) and Faculty of Economics, Thammasat University.

OFFICIAL LANGUAGE
English.

CONFERENCE SCOPE
(1) The SIBR Conference invites submission of academic and professional research papers/abstracts from the full range of business and economics disciplines, including all sub-fields and related topics in Economics, Accounting, Finance, Marketing, Management, and Business Ethics. Research papers/abstracts cutting across business and non-business disciplines (e.g., education, engineering, law, politics, psychology, sociology, etc.) are also welcome.

(2) The SIBR Conference encourages discussions on research-in-progress. For those authors who cannot submit full papers, they can present their latest research

findings at the SIBR Conference if their abstracts are accepted. Peer reviewed abstracts will be published in the conference proceedings.

(3) Interested parties without papers/abstracts for presentation are also invited to participate as attendees at the SIBR Conference.

SUBMISSION GUIDELINES

(1) Submit full paper/abstract (in MS Word) via the Online Submission.

(2) Full papers/abstracts received by the deadline will be (double-blind) peer-reviewed by an internal panel on a rolling basis. A notification of acceptance/rejection will be issued within 14 days after submission.

(3) For co-authored papers/abstracts (with more than one author), the submitting author will serve as the corresponding author who has the responsibility to forward all correspondences to his/her co-authors (e.g., acceptance/rejection emails).

PUBLICATION

(1) Full papers/abstracts accepted for the SIBR Conference will be included in the Conference Proceedings (ISSN: 2223-5078) for free distribution at the conference. Authors are NOT required to transfer copyrights to SIBR.

(2) Several journals (indexed by Scopus, ProQuest, EconLit, etc.) will publish special issues featuring selected papers from the SIBR Conference:

- Review of Integrative Business and Economics Research (RIBER) — papers accepted for RIBER will be nominated for the "RIBER Best Paper Prize". See point (1) in the next section on BEST PAPER PRIZES & AWARDS.
- International Journal of Trade and Global Markets.
- International Journal of Economic Policy in Emerging Economies.
- International Journal of Monetary Economics and Finance, etc.

Upon submitting to the SIBR conference for presentation, the authors will be invited to choose a journal as a possible publication outlet. Final acceptance is subject to further editorial review. There is NO extra publication fee.

BEST PAPER PRIZES & AWARDS

(1) RIBER Best Paper Prize: All SIBR Conference papers published at Review of Integrative Business and Economics Research (RIBER) will be nominated for the

Unit 1　Preparations for International Conference

RIBER Best Paper Prize, which serves to celebrate and applaud the best TWO papers in each issue of the journal for their significant contribution to interdisciplinary research. The winners will receive a cash prize of USD100 during their attendance of the next SIBR Conference within 12 months after the date of the current conference (the prize will be shared by the authors of a co-authored paper). The results will be announced within 2 months after the publication of each issue. This prize is NOT in conjunction with the SIBR Best Paper Award.

(2) SIBR Best Paper Award: Approximately 10% of the papers accepted for presentation at the conference will be selected as best papers for their outstanding contributions to interdisciplinary research. A Best Paper Award certificate will be issued to the award-winning authors.

IMPORTANT DATES

　　Deadline for submission of paper/abstract: April 19th, 2019 (extended)
　　Notification of acceptance/rejection: Within 14 days after submission
　　Deadline for early-bird registration: April 26th, 2019
　　Conference date: June 9th - 10th, 2019

REGISTRATION FEE

All conference participants must pay the registration fee. For each paper/abstract, at least one author must attend and pay the registration fee. For all participants with or without papers/abstracts for presentation at the SIBR Conference, the registration fee is

　　Early-bird Registration Fee (on or before April 26th, 2019) HKD 2,550 (approx. USD 330);

　　Regular Registration Fee (after April 26th, 2019) HKD 3,100 (approx. USD 400).

TERMS & CONDITIONS:

　　1. The registration fee includes: conference attendance and luncheon (2 days), SIBR Conference Proceedings (on USB drive), certificate of attendance, and official receipt.

　　2. If the same attending author will present more than one paper, the fee for each additional paper is HKD 775 (approx. USD 100).

3. If your paper is multi-authored and more than one author will attend the conference, each attending author needs to register separately and pay individual registration fee separately.

4. The registration fee does NOT include hotel accommodation and transport.

5. For cancellations made before the early-bird registration deadline, the registration fee is refundable after deducting USD 100 administrative charge. The registration fee is non-refundable for cancellations made on and after the early-bird registration deadline.

ENQUIRY

Please contact the conference secretariat at secretary@sibresearch.org.

Check your understanding

(1) What are the topics of the conference?

(2) What are the paper submission requirements?

(3) List related information about publication.

Useful Expressions and Sentence Patterns

1. To inform of the background, sponsors (or organizers), name, venue, date, etc. of the conference

(1) The conference will be held at the University of Victoria, Victoria, B. C., Canada, August 22-24, 2006.

(2) The IEEE International Conference on Cloud Computing Technology & Science 2015 will be the 7th in the series of conferences, steered by the Cloud Computing Association, that brings together researchers, developers and users interested in cloud computing systems to present and discuss the needs of, and innovations in, the area.

(3) An international conference on the Constitution and Education will be hosted by the Faculty of Education Sciences, North-West University, Potchefstroom Campus, South Africa.

Unit 1 Preparations for International Conference

2. To introduce information about conference scope

(1) The conference will aim to provide a forum for researchers, academics and industrialists to share their up to date findings and achievements in the fields of design and manufacture.

(2) It will provide a unified communication platform for researchers in a wide area of topics from Materials for Sustainable Society, … and other related fields.

(3) Five simultaneous conference tracks will be held, covering different aspects of Enterprise Information Systems Application, including Enterprise Database Technology, …

(4) ICCAD (2006) serves EDA & Design professionals, highlighting new challenges and innovative solutions for Integrated-Circuit Design Technologies and Systems.

3. To introduce the conference agenda

(1) The first day will consist of an exhibition and demonstration of new, innovative wireless technologies, devices and applications. The second day will feature panel discussions on unlicensed wireless technologies.

(2) The conference will begin with registration and reception on Thursday, August 22.

(3) The final session of the conference will be brought forward from Friday to Tuesday.

(4) The conference format will begin with tutorials and workshops on the morning of Sunday, November 4. The formal scientific sessions will begin on Monday, November 5, at 8:30 AM and end at noon Wednesday, November 7.

(5) The Conference will run over three days and features presentations by authors of all accepted papers, as well as keynote lecturers.

4. To introduce information about other activities at the conference

(1) Supported by the EU Asia-Link program, a Postgraduate School will be held pre and during the conference (6th -10th January 2006).

(2) The Conference will organize a tour to the "Ice and Snow Grand World", which is regarded as the "Disney Land" of ice and snow. It is part of the "Harbin International Ice and Snow Festival", one of the four largest winter festivals in the

world.

(3) ICNC' 06-FSKD, the joint conferences will feature plenary speeches given by worldwide renowned scholars, regular sessions with broad coverage, and some special sessions focused on cross-fertilization over these exciting and yet closely-related areas.

5. To introduce information about paper submission

(1) Potential authors are invited to submit abstracts of about 300 words to adm2006@ntu.ac.uk.

(2) The authors of accepted abstracts will be asked to submit full papers which will be refered for conference presentation.

(3) All paper submissions should follow the IEEE 8.5"×11" Two-Column Format. Each submission can have 10 pages. An appendix of 2 pages maximum is also allowed.

(4) Papers should be original and not be submitted in parallel to any other conference or journal. Papers should include the full author list before the submission deadline.

(5) Authors should submit a paper in English of up to 8 A4 pages, carefully checked for correct grammar and spelling, using the submission procedure indicated below.

(6) 5 A4 pages (including figures) version of the paper, using the templates that can be downloaded below. The paper must contain enough information for the TPC and reviewers to judge on the originality and quality of the work.

5. To introduce information about the review and publication of the submitted papers

(1) Selected papers (up to 35%) from the Proceedings will be considered for publication in refereed journals (EI/SCI Indexed) and the Lecture Notes of Computer Science, Springer Verlag (SCI Indexed) subject to extensive revision.

(2) All ICMMS 2018 accepted papers will be published by the international journal Applied Mechanics and Materials (ISSN: 1660-9336), which will be indexed by Elsevier: SCOPUS www.scopus.com and EI Compendex www.ei.org/.

(3) The program committee will review all papers and the author of each paper

will be notified of the result, by email.

(4) A "blind" paper evaluation method will be used.

(5) Acceptance will be based on quality, relevance and originality.

(6) Full-length papers submitted to the conference by the deadline will be reviewed by a panel of experts and judged on quality, originality, clarity and topical content.

6. Notification of acceptance and refusal

(1) Receipt of paper submission will be confirmed by email.

(2) Submissions received after this date will not be given primary consideration.

(3) Acceptance of the paper will be confirmed by JICC 2011 Program Committee based on content quality of the extended abstract.

(4) Late registration fees or paper submissions will result in papers being excluded from the conference proceedings.

7. To introduce information about registration fees and expenses

(1) We will cover the costs of all the invited presenters after arrival at the conference in Beijing.

(2) The costs of invited non-presenter participants will also be covered, but a 300 RMB registration fee will be required.

(3) Anticipated conference fee (US$258) includes evening reception at the architecture Center on Friday, the Perrault lecture, three-course lunch and refreshments at Pembroke College, and optional Sunday tour of new Cambridge libraries given by Eastern Region Architects.

(4) The organizing committee will pay for the food, boarding and visiting fees spent from August 16 to 23. Participants need to pay other fees not mentioned above.

Task 4: Conference Agenda/ Programs

General Knowledge

Agenda means a list of the business or subject to be considered at a meeting. It must be prepared before a meeting and it is supposed to be well-kept in a file for future reference. No matter what kind of a meeting is held, secretaries are to prepare the agenda.

A Conference Program is made after the academic committee of a conference decides whose papers can be presented at the conference. It serves as a guide as well as a plan for the participants. It usually lists all the activities to be done at the conference. Meanwhile, it gives the definite time and place when and whereas particular activity takes place. Therefore, a Conference Program usually contains information about time, dates, activities, place, people involved, etc.

Sample Demonstration

2017年国际分析科学大会（ICAS 2017）会议日程

Opening & Plenary Lectures		
6th May, 2007 Functional Hall, HICEC, Haikou, China		
08:30-09:30 Ceremony		
Chair	Jin-Ming Lin, Tsinghua University, China Secretary General of the Mass Analysis Committee, Chinese Chemical Society	
Welcome address	08:30-08:40	Erkang Wang, Changchun, Institute of Applied Chemistry, CAS Honorary Chairman of ICAS2017, International Advisory Board of IUPAC International Congress on Analytical Science
	08:40-08:50	Xiurong Yang, Changchun Institute of Applied Chemistry, CAS Chair of the Analytical Chemistry Committee, Chinese Chemical Society
	08:50-08:55	Qinghua Fan, Secretary General of Chinese Chemical Society
	08:55-09:00	Shiwen Sun, Vice mayor of the Haikou Municipal People's Government
Opening Performances	09:00-09:20	Hainan Normal University

Unit 1　Preparations for International Conference

09:30-12:10 Plenary Lectures		
Chairs	Hongyuan Chen, Nanjing University, China Li-Jun Wan, Institute of Chemistry, CAS & University of Science and Technology of China, China	
PL-1	09:30-10:10	Takenhiko Kitamorl	Extended Nanofluidics as a Promising Platform for single Cell Molecule Analysis
PL-2	10:10-10:50	Benzhong Tang	Wonder Science of AIE, Advanced Tools Based AIEgens
PL-3	10:50-11:30	Aldo Roda	A general presentation of the use of smartphone as a portable analytical device covering the most actual concept and applications
PL-4	11:30-12:10	Xinrong Zhang	Mass Spectrometry-Based Single-Cell Analysis: A New Frontier in Metabolomics

Scientific Program for Oral Presentations		
Session 1 Optical Spectroscopic Analysis (OS)		
Room: Functional Hall B		
6th May (Sat.)		
Chairs	Bin Ren, Xiamen University, China Juyong Yoon, Ewha Woman's University, Korea	
13:30-14:00	6P-OS-K1	High Efficiency Organic Solar Cells Based on Absorption-Complementary Donor and Acceptor Photovoltaic Materials Yongfang Li, Institute of Chemistry, China
14:00-14:30	6P-OS-K2	Fluorescent Probes and Activable photosensitizers Juyong Yoon, Ewha Woman's University, Korea
...	...	...
15:10-15:30	6P-OS-I3	...
Coffee Break		
Poster Presentation, 15:50-17:50,Poster Lobby		
Dinner		

Useful Expressions

About related people:

preparatory committee	sponsor	organizer	participant
organizing committee	keynote speaker	contact person	session chair
program committee	co-sponsor	honorary chairman	members
executive secretary	chairman	vice chairman	plenary lecturer

About presentation:

opening remarks	opening speech	opening address	report
welcome speech	keynote speech	presentation	session
paper session	poster session	demonstration	paper
question and answer period	closing speech	closing remarks	closing address

About reception:

lunch	coffee or tea break	reception	banquet
dinner	tour and sightseeing	dinner speech	

Unit 2

International Letter Exchange

Learning Objectives

In this unit, you will learn to accomplish the following tasks:

- Task 1: To familiarize the format of a business letter
- Task 2: To write a letter of invitation
- Task 3: To write a letter of reply

Task 1: Business Letters

What Are Business Letters?

A business letter, by definition, is a letter written in the formal language, usually used when writing from one business organization to another, or for correspondence between such organizations and their customers, clients and other external parties.

There are two kinds of letters, formal letters and informal letters. A formal letter is a type of letter articulating formal note, and it is used mostly for business purposes, in correspondence, when submitting requests, making complaints, etc. Formal letters are written mostly in cases when your correspondent is someone you do not know in person, however, except in business, when it is used to preserve business practice.

Format of Business Letters

1. Letterhead
2. Dates
3. Inside address
4. Salutation
5. Body
6. Complimentary close
7. Signature

1. Letterhead

The letterhead is also called return address, which is the full address of the writer. It is typed in the upper right- hand corner of the first page. In the business world, letterhead is normally printed on the top of the letter paper in the middle. Thus you need not write it again. Just write the date. For a personal letter, you also need not write the letterhead.

Unit 2 International Letter Exchange

Notes for letterhead: You should be aware of the order you write. Letterhead is just reversed from that in Chinese, i.e., from the smallest unit to the biggest unit. For example, the number of the room, name of the building, name of the street, city, province and then the country.

(1) School of Law.
   Shandong University
   27 Shanda Nanlu
   Jinan, Shandong 250100
   P.R. China

(2) School of Materials Engineering.
   Purdue University
   Neil Armstrong Hall of Engineering
   701 West Stadium Avenue
   Lafayette, Indiana 47907-2045
   Phone: +1-765-494-4103
   Fax: +1-765-494-1204

2. Dates

The date is typed a few lines below the last line of the letterhead. The format of the dateline differs from country to country. The common formats are typical American one (Month/Day/Year) and British one (Day/Month/Year).

British style: 18 May, 2014   18th March, 2014   (day-month-year)
American style: May 18, 2014   March 18th, 2014   (month-day-year)

3. Inside address

Inside address is the address exactly the same as that on the envelope. The opening goes above the salutation on the left, which is always omitted in personal letters. The order of the inside address is the same as the order of letterhead. While in the business world, if you know the receivers' name and position, you should write them before the company name and address.

(1) Professor George Smith.
   School of Mathematical Sciences
   University of Nottingham
   University Park

Nottingham

NG7 2RD UK

(2) Mr. John Smith.

Broadcasting Center

114 course Drive

Iowa City, IA 21002

USA

- Some abbreviations of the mailing address

Dept. = Department	Inst. = Institute	Str. = Street
Univ. = University	Bldg. = Building	Ave. = Avenue
Rd. = Road	W. = West	E. = East
N. = North	S. = South	

- Titles of the recipient

  courtesy title — Mrs.   Ms.   Miss   Mr.

  professional title — Dr.   Professor

  business title — Manager Director

4. Salutation

The salutation is the greeting, which goes one or two spaces below the opening at the left-hand margin. Usually, it is best to say "Dear…" if you know the name of the receiver, or just "Dear Sir/Madam" if you do not know the receiver's name. Then you should use a comma (,) or nothing.

Note: In China, people always address the title of one's position, such as manager, director, and teacher, etc. In English, however, these are not addressing. It is not correctly used that you write "Dear Teacher Zhang", "Dear Manager Yang", and so on.

British style	American style
Dear Mr. Johnson,	Dear President Fang
Dear Dr. Lee,	Dear Professor Stone

If the letter is to an organization or to persons whose names you do not know, the following greetings are used:

Dear Sir,	Dear Sir
Dear Madam,	Dear Madam

Unit 2 International Letter Exchange

Dear Sir or Madam,   Dear Sir or Madam
To whom it may concern,   To whom it may concern
Dear Colleague,   Dear Colleague

5. Body

It is the most important part of the letter — the content of the letter. It is one or two spaces below the salutation. The paragraph should be blocked or indented, according to the style chosen. Usually, it is single spaced for a business letter.

It is the most important part of the letter, which expresses the message you want to send and you should stick to your point. The opening paragraph should introduce the subject or purpose of the letter, and the closing paragraph should inquire what action or response is desired or emphasize the action that had been or will be taken.

- First paragraph:

The first paragraph should be short and state the purpose of the letter — to make an inquiry, complain, request something, etc.

- Middle paragraph(s):

The paragraph or paragraphs in the middle of the letter should contain the relevant information behind the writing of the letter. Most letters in English are not very long, so keep the information to the essentials and concentrate on organizing it in a clear and logical manner rather than expanding too much.

- Last Paragraph:

The last paragraph of a formal letter should state what action you expect the recipient to take—to refund, send you information, etc.

6. Complimentary close

It is the way of saying goodbye. There are various words to choose in English closing. It should match the tone established by the salutation and carried through the body of the letter. It is usually two spaces below the body of the letter, together with the signature group. If you use a comma (,) after the salutation, you should use a comma after the closing. If you use nothing after the salutation, you also should use nothing after the closing.

(1) Formal closes.

British Style   American Style

Yours sincerely,   Sincerely yours

Yours respectfully,   Respectfully yours

Yours truly,   Very truly yours

Yours cordially,   Cordially yours

(2) Informal closes (often in emails).

Best regards,   Best wishes,   With best wishes,

All the best,   With respect,   With kind regards,

Yours,   Love,

7. Signature

The signature is the last part of a letter. In business letters, you should sign your full name. Your name should be typed also in another line. However, in personal letters, you can sign your full name, first name or nickname according to the relationship with the receivers.

Eg:

John Lee

Dean & Professor of biology

Presley University

8. Enclosure/ P. S. (postscript)/copies

This should be located at the bottom of the paper.

(1) Enclosure.

It is used to indicate that something other than the letter has been enclosed within the letter. It can be such things as a resume, a photo, a check or a receipt, etc.. Write Enclosure or Enc. to remind the addressee. It is often written one or two spaces below the signature to the left margin of the bottom of the letter.

(2) Postscript (P.S.).

It brings up a short addition to a letter. If you have something additional to say after you have finished the letter, you may begin with P.S. (common and acceptable). While using P.S., it is not advisable to use it in a formal letter, since it tends to give readers an impression that you seem to have not given the letter thorough thought.

(3) Copies (c.c.).

If you send a copy of your letter to someone other than the recipient, write "c.c.", which stands for copy/copies circulated. It is often used in inter-office letters.

eg. c.c. Dr. Clark James, Dean
    c.c. Dr. Bill Max,   Program Director

⌛ Two Styles of Format

There are two styles of composing letters. One is the indented style, and the other is the block style. Nowadays, the block style is more popular, especially in the business world.

1. Full block format

This format is very modern. Every line of the letter begins at the left margin (flush left), with a space of one line between paragraphs.

2. Modified block format with indented paragraphs

Different from the full block format, this format places the date and the complimentary close near the right margin. And the first line of each paragraph is indented, with no space of one line between paragraphs.

Rules for Writing Business Letters

Business letters play an important role in the development of friendly trade relationships. The most effective letter should be easy to read and easy to understand.

Generally speaking, business letter writing follows the rules of 7Cs, that is, consideration, completeness, correctness, concreteness, conciseness, clarity and courtesy.

1. Consideration

Consideration means trying to put yourself in his or her place, to give consideration to his or her wishes, demands, interests and difficulties.

2. Correctness

Correctness means giving factual information, accurate figures and exact terms in writing business letters. The rule of correctness seems especially important when business letters involve the right, the duties and the interest of both sides.

Therefore we should not understate nor overstate as understatement might lead to less confidence and hold up the trade development, while overstatement throws you into an awkward position.

3. Completeness

Completeness means all the necessary information is conveyed in business letters and all the composing parts are included.

4. Concreteness

Concreteness means what the letter says should be specific, definite rather than vague, abstract and general, for vague or general information can cause ambiguity or even disputes.

5. Conciseness

Conciseness means complete message but briefest expression with no sacrificing clarity or courtesy. A good business letter should be precise and to the point. Generally speaking, single words are more efficient than phrases.

6. Clarity

Clarity means you express yourself clearly and logically in the simplest language, for plain, simple words are more easily understood and logical arrangement of the information is easy to follow.

7. Courtesy

Courtesy means to show tactfully in your letters the honest friendship, thoughtful appreciation, sincere politeness, considerate understanding, and heartfelt respect.

Sample Demonstration

Sample 1   Letter of Complaint

May 4, 2002

Dear Sir/Madam,

Further to my telephone call this morning, I would like to write to you for the tape-recorder I bought last month in your shop.

I just used it only for a week when it broke. I took it to a local repair shop, but they told us that it was a factory defect and suggested that I take it to your branch company in our town. I waited for more than two weeks, and your company did not send a replacement.

I will be grateful if you could replace the machine for me soon.

Yours faithfully,
James Christopher
James Christopher

Sample 2   Letter of Apology

Dear Customer,

I am writing to you to explain the reasons for the poor service we have given over the past few months. I apologize for the incomplete delivery and no replies to the inquiries. I am extremely sorry for all the inconvenience caused by our poor services.

The main reasons lie in our working procedures which have not kept pace with the expansion of our company. First of all, we do not have enough staff to deal with the deliveries and inquiries; secondly, our warehouse is not large enough to store our goods; thirdly, our computer systems are also not so modern as to satisfy the need of company's expansion.

I promise that orders will surely be delivered promptly and correctly. See to it that we have already taken some actions. Now we have already invited more staff, and we have already rented a warehouse acquired. Moreover, we have already invested enough money to improve the computer system to cope with the pace of the expansion. Accordingly, the poor services as before will not appear anymore.

Yours faithfully,
Henry
Henry, the manager

Unit 2 International Letter Exchange

Sample 3 Letter of Congratulations

Dear Holly,

I was pleased to hear that you have been promoted to General manager of ACE company. This news came as no surprise to me; I always consider you as a person who was going places! I am very happy to see your abilities recognized — I know you will do an excellent job in your new position.

Please accept my sincere personal congratulations. I am so happy for your good future.

Sincerely yours,
Mary
Mary

Task 2: Letters of Invitation

General Introduction

1. What are invitation letters?

Before the international conference, the conference host or organizer(s) will send invitation letters to famous scholars and experts in the field and invite them as keynote speakers to the conference. They will also invite other prospective authors to present their new ideas, valuable works, and ongoing research at the conference. These letters are formal letters and therefore should bear all the necessary information about the occasion(s), and express the host's sincerity and hospitality toward the attendees. Before drafting the letter, first seriously think about the event, and it should have all the relevant facts.

The invitation letter for a meeting should follow the regular layout in the header. It should contain the address of the sender and recipient. It is recommended that your invitation letter for meeting deliver a clear message, and therefore try to keep it short and concise. The ending of this formal letter should vary, depending on the type of relationship you have with the recipient.

2. Format of invitation letters

- Letterhead: the address of the writer
- Date of writing
- Inside address: the name and address of the recipient
- Salutation
- Body of the letter:
  the name of the conference, time and venue
  the purpose of the invitation
  the conference theme/ arrangement
  contact information
  the anticipated pleasure in meeting the recipient(s)
- Complimentary close
- Signature

Unit 2 International Letter Exchange

- Enclosure (if any)

3. Tips

- Make sure invitation letters are cordial and enthusiastic
- Extend the invitation before going into the details of the conference/Give a brief account of the relevant details
- Give the name of the conference, the time and the venue at the beginning
- Do not use abbreviations in formal invitations
- Include any accommodations that will be made
- Give the name of the contact person along with the phone number
- If you invite someone to speak at a conference, you should also mention the type of speech, the topic or the scope and how long the speech will be
- If a reply is required, place R.S.V.P. at the end of the invitation, often at the left corner
- Check your letter for typos or any other mistakes in language
- Keep the letter concise, factual, and to the point with a polite tone
- Use language and terminology familiar to the intended recipients

Sample Demonstration

Sample 1:

Invitation Letter for the 14th Canadian Collaborative Mental Health Care Conference

---

Dear Mr. Wu Jing,

We are pleased to invite you to attend the 14th Canadian Collaborative Mental Health Care Conference (14th CCMHCC) to be held on Thursday, June 27 and Friday, June 28, 2013. Montreal has been selected as the host city. This annual event will take place at the Delta Centre-Ville Hotel, a downtown location within easy walking distance of the Old City. You will be charmed by the unique character of the city of Montreal, the metropolis of the province of Quebec. For those of you who wish to extend your stay, you can combine business and pleasure by attending the 34th edition of the famous International Jazz Festival of Montreal that will begin on Friday, June 28th and continue for the next 10 days.

The 14th CCMHCC is organized by the Canadian Psychiatric Association and the College of Family Physicians of Canada Collaborative Working Group on Shared Mental Health Care. This conference will take on a bilingual character, in French and in English, and simultaneous translation will be available for the main speeches and presentations. This is a unique opportunity to bring together people who are involved in collaborative mental health care and to create links that consolidate and enrich the networks among these stakeholders. We are expecting over 300 delegates from Quebec in Canada and the international community. The interest in collaborative mental health care is shared by a wide audience, including particularly individuals living with a mental disorder and their families, healthcare professionals from different backgrounds, managers and decision makers, community groups working in the field, physicians (including family physicians, pediatricians and psychiatrists), teachers from academic departments, researchers and collaborators from different sectors (e.g., emergency social services, law enforcement officers, or employers).

This conference will provide an additional impetus to collaborative care, an irresistible movement which redesigns the healthcare system in order to adapt it to the realities of the 21st century. The theme of the conference, Collaboration and Complexity: Seeking Out New Forms of Life, illustrates the emerging nature of the strategic vision of collaborative care, sets the clinical operations within a complex context which fits in the postmodern societal model and points out its profound innovative potential.

We invite sponsorship support to help make this conference a success. There are several ways to help; additional information will be provided shortly.

We look forward to welcoming you to Montreal.

Sincerely yours,
(signature)
Michel Gervais
Chair of the 14th CCMHCC

Sample 2:

Dear Ms Wang,

I have the great pleasure, on behalf of the International Conference on Medical Biometrics Organization, of inviting you to contribute to the symposium on medical device technologies, medical data processing and management, medical pattern recognition, medical biometric systems and applications to be held in Shenzhen, between 30th May and 1st June 2014.

We would like to invite you to submit a manuscript to the International Conference on medical imaging devices, medical information retrieval, biometric technologies, feature matching and classification, computer-aided diagnosis and other applications. The idea is to present originally contributed research, review, and short communication articles in the field

Unit 2 International Letter Exchange

of medical biometrics. Deadline for submissions would be April 3, 2014. Kindly submit your manuscripts as an E-mail attachment at luguangm@hit.edu.cn.

I will be looking forward to your favorable reply.

Sincerely yours,
(signiture)
Guangming Lu

Sample 3:

Dear Professor Wang,

On behalf of the Ohio State University, I would be very pleased to invite you to attend and chair the 2004 International Conference on Data Processing to be held in Michigan, from October 25 to October 28, 2004.

You are an internationally acclaimed scholar and educator. Your participation will be among the highlights of the Conference.

We sincerely hope that you could accept our invitation. As you know, this is the 10th anniversary of the conference and we plan to make it a truly international meeting. We have accepted many papers from several foreign countries, including two from China.

If you can come, please let us know as soon as possible, since we have to prepare the final program soon. We are looking forward to your acceptance.

Sincerely yours,
(signature)
Peter White

⧖ Useful Expressions

1. Extending invitation:

(1) It is my pleasure to invite you to attend (*the 14th Canadian Collaborative Mental Health Care Conference (14th CCMHCC)*) to be held in (*Montreal, Canada,*) on (*Thursday, June 27*) and (*Friday, June 28, 2013*).

(2) It is with great pleasure that I invite you to the (*fifth Annual Computer Conference*). This year's conference will be held at (*Xi' an*), from (*July 23rd to July 26th, 2013*).

(3) Considering your expertise in this field, the Organizing Committee is very pleased to invite you to be the keynote speaker in the Plenary Session of (*the International Symposium on English Learning and Teaching at Tertiary Level in the Chinese Context*) to be held in (*Nanjing, July 17-19, 2013*).

(4) It is my pleasure, on behalf of the Organizing Committee, to invite you to attend and chair a session of (*the 19th International Conference on Chemical Education (19th ICCE)*), to be held in upcoming (*August 12-17, 2006,*) in (*Seoul, the Republic of Korea*).

(5) As co-chair of the (*40th Annual Meeting of the Association for Computational Linguistics*), to be held in (*Hong Kong October 10-25, 2014*), I am writing to ask whether you would be willing to present a talk in English at the conference as an invited speaker.

2. Expecting attendance:

(1) We sincerely hope that you can accept this invitation.

(2) I would like to take this opportunity to strongly encourage you to attend this very important session.

(3) I do hope you can make time in your busy schedule to attend the conference and share your ideas on this topic on the panel.

(4) This Conference Committee and I hope you will find your conference day educational and rewarding.

(5) I look forward to the active participation of your organization at this important event in (*July*).

(6) We are looking forward to seeing you in (*Seoul*).

3. Meals and accommodation

(1) You will be provided with a subsistence allowance and accommodation for the duration of the conference.

(2) If you can come to the symposium, your local expenses, including hotel accommodations, meals, and the conference fee will be covered by the organizers.

(3) The *(CE)* would provide the cost of an economy class airfare from *(Beijing)* to the conference, hotel accommodations during the conference, and free registration to the conference.

(4) Our department offers a fee and will, of course, reimburse your traveling and hotel expenses.

(5) Your round-trip air ticket and meal expenses will be subsidized.

4. Others

(1) We enclose a copy of the advance notice of the conference.

(2) Please find enclosed information on accommodations, transportation, and registration.

(3) For more details of the conference, please refer to/go to the conference website: (*http://temasek.nus.edu.2005*).

(4) If you have any inquires or need any assistance, please do not hesitate to contact (*Cherylene Hidano, Program Officer*…at *808-944-7338*), or email …at (*hidanoc@eastwest center.org*).

Task 3: Letters of Reply

General Introduction

1. What are letters of acceptance or refusal?

An acceptance or refusal letter is sent in response to a job offer or academic research and is a formal statement of your acceptance or refusal of the offer.

2. Format of letters of acceptance or refusal

(1) Format of letters of acceptance.
- Letterhead the address of the writer
- Date of writing
- Inside address: the name and address of the recipient
- Salutation
- Body of the letter:
    expressing your pleasure and honor at being invited
    repeating the main content, date, time, venue
    agreeing to do what was asked
    closing the letter with your thanks, good wishes, etc
- Complimentary close
- Signature
- Enclosure (if any)

(2) Format of letters of refusal.
- Letterhead the address of the writer
- Date of writing
- Inside address: the name and address of the recipient
- Salutation
- Body of the letter:
    expressing your pleasure and honor at being invited
    repeating the main content, date, time, venue
    expressing your regrets
    giving convincing reasons for your refusal
    extending good wishes

Unit 2　International Letter Exchange

- Complimentary close
- Signature
- Enclosure (if any)

3. Tips

(1) Tips of letters of acceptance.

- Express thanks at the beginning or at the end of the first paragraph.
- State contents briefly.
- Inquire about particular information: accommodations; equipment for your speech.
- Avoid ungracious amplifications.

(2) Tips of letters of refusal.

- Express thanks at the beginning or at the end of the first paragraph.
- Make a courteous, sincere remark, and present convincing reasons for declining the invitation.
- Suggest any alternative courses of action or other resources, if appropriate.
- Express good wishes for the next cooperation in the future.

Sample Demonstration

Sample 1　A Letter of Acceptance of Invitation

> Center of English Language Education
> The University of Nottingham,
> University Park,
> Nottingham.
> NG7 2RD. UK
> April 12, 2014
>
> Ms. Hilary Zhang on Conference Convener,
> Language Center
> The Hong Kong University of Science and Technology,
> Clear Water Bay, Kowloon,
> Hong Kong

Dear Ms. Hilary Zhang,

I have received your letter dated April 1, 2014, inviting me to attend the conference on "The Autonomy and Language Learning: Maintaining Control" to be held in International Conference Center of the Hong Kong University of Science and Technology in Hong Kong, June 25, 2014. Thank you for your kind invitation.

I am pleased to accept your invitation and will send my paper entitled *The Importance of Maintaining Control in Language Learning* to the Paper Committee before the required date.

Thank you once again for your kind invitation and for your effort in making the conference a successful one. I am looking forward to meeting you soon in Hong Kong.

Faithfully yours,

(signature)

John Smith

Sample 2 A Letter of Declination for Invitation

School of Mathematical Sciences

The University of Nottingham

University Park

Nottingham NG7 2RD UK

March 20, 2013

Mr. Li Donglin

School of Mathematics and System Science

Shandong University

27 Shanda Nanlu

Jinan, Shandong 250100

P. R. China

Dear Mr. Li Donglin,

Many thanks for your letter of 18th March 2013, inviting me to attend and chair a session of the forthcoming the twelfth International Conference on Finite or Infinite Dimensional Complex Analysis to be held from July 24 to 28, 2013 in Jinan and Taian city, China.

Much to my regret, I shall not be able to honor the invitation because I have been suffering from ill health this spring. I am firmly advised that it would be unwise to undertake any distant travel in the near future.

Unit 2　International Letter Exchange

> I feel very sorry to miss the opportunity of meeting you and many of other colleagues in the field of Mathematics.
>
> I wish the conference a complete success.
>
> Truly yours,
(signature)
George Smith

Useful Expressions

1. Expressions used in letters of acceptance of invitation

(1) I am pleased to accept your invitation and will send my paper entitled (*The Importance of Maintaining Control in Language Learning*) to the Paper Committee before the required date.

(2) I have received your letter dated June 22, inviting me to speak at the (*Opening Ceremony of the Fifth National Council Meeting of Translators Association of China*) to be held on (*November 4-6*), in (*Beijing*). I will speak on (*Globalization and Diversity: What Do They Mean for Translators?*). Thank you for your kind invitation.

(3) Thank you for your letter *of June* 23. I am pleased to confirm my participation in this year's conference in (*September*).

(4) I am pleased to take part in the conference and look forward to it with pleasure.

(5) I look forward to visiting (*London*) and to seeing you again at the conference this (*September*).

(6) I would be grateful if you could send me further details about the program.

(7) Thank you once again for your kind invitation and for your effort in making the conference a successful one.

(8) I am looking forward to meeting you soon in (*Montreal*).

2. Expressions used in letters of declining invitation

(1) Much to my regret, I shall not be able to honor the invitation because (*I have been suffering from ill health this spring*).

· 43 ·

(2) I feel very sorry to miss the opportunity of meeting you and many other colleagues in the field of (*Dimensional Complex Analysis*).

(3) Unfortunately, I have a previous commitment and thus can not help this time. I would be happy to speak if you would give me another opportunity at some other time.

(4) Much to my regret, I shall not attend the conference because I have to chair a meeting to be held in (*France*) at that time.

(5) I am very sorry to inform you that I will be unable to go to (*Canada*). I just have learned that the special flight that I had planned to take has been canceled and the cost of a regular airline fare is prohibitive.

(6) Unfortunately, I will not be able to give an update on last time's presentation. Please accept my sincere apologies, and I hope you will think of me again if the WCA needs a guest speaker at some future date.

(7) I feel very sorry to miss the opportunity of meeting you and many other colleagues in the field of (*Knowledge Economy*). I wish the conference a complete success.

(8) However, I look forward to attending the conference next year.

Unit 3

Academic Paper Writing

Learning Objectives

In this unit, you will learn to accomplish the following tasks:

➢ Task 1: To know general knowledge of academic papers
➢ Task 2: To write Title
➢ Task 3: To write Abstract
➢ Task 4: To organize Body of an academic paper, including:
   Introduction
   Literature Review
   Material and Methods
   Results
   Discussions
   Conclusion
➢ Task 5: To familiarize Acknowledgement, References, Notes
➢ Task 6: To avoid errors in academic writings

Task 1: General Knowledge of Academic Papers

A critical aspect of the scientific process is the reporting of new results in scientific journals in order to disseminate that information to the larger community of scientists. Then, that is a scientific paper! *A scientific paper is a written report describing original research results. Papers are a central part of research.* If your research does not generate papers, it might just as well not have been done. "Interesting and unpublished" is equivalent to "non-existent". How to write English academic papers for international professional publication has become a major concern for Chinese academics. In this unit, issues relevant to the actual paper writing will be discussed in detail.

Most journals accept papers for publication only after peer review by a small group of scientists who work in the same field and who recommend the paper be published. Mastery of the appropriate format will enable you to adapt easily to most journals. It is not sufficient, by learning such format mentioned in this unit, to make you an accomplished writer. All journals have a set of instructions for authors which explicitly state how their paper should be formatted for submission. Consider this guide to be your instructions when writing.

1. Classification of professional papers

Professional papers assigned in universities and colleges or any other research institutions are generally of the following four types: "report paper", "research paper", "course paper", "thesis paper".

(1) Report paper

The report paper summarizes and reports the findings of the author(s) on a particular subject. The author(s) may not give his/her/their own opinion on the issue, nor evaluates the findings, but merely catalogs them in a sensible sequence.

(2) Research paper

A research paper can be intelligent, well-informed, interesting, and original in its conclusion. It draws its material from many sources. Its aim is to assemble facts and ideas and by studying them to draw new conclusions as to facts or interpretations, or to present the material in the light of a new interest.

(3) Course paper

A course paper mainly refers to the paper written after a specific course is learnt or at the end of the term. So its contents usually should be in line with the course requirements and under the instruction of the course instructor.

(4) Thesis paper (dissertation)

A thesis paper is usually written and submitted in partial fulfillment of the requirements for the degree of MA or MS (or Ph.D) in a specific discipline. A thesis is a proposition that the writer is willing to argue against or defend. Writing a thesis paper requires the writer to exercise judgment, evaluate evidence, and construct logical argument. The thesis, or dissertation, should be independently completed, under the supervisor's guidance, by the candidate himself/herself, reflecting the candidate's own research findings.

2. Ways of preparing professional papers

There are six steps involved in writing research papers:

Step 1: Select a subject

According to some experienced authors, one-third or even half of their time would have to be spent on searching for good ideas or subjects in order to make their research really valuable.

Step 2: Finding topics

It should be a topic:

- Within the reach of the author and capable of being finished within the assigned time limit.
- Of practical value for the specialty or the development of science in general.
- For which sufficient materials and documents can be made available either through readings or through investigations.
- Free from the author's personal bias.
- Bears being tested theoretically and experimentally.

Step 3: Outline the paper

Your outline also should reflect the organizational format you have chosen for your paper.

- Write a thesis statement that summarizes the main point you want to make on the topic.
- Create subheadings for all the main headings in your outline.
- Create further subdivisions within your outline as necessary.
- Add a conclusion that summarizes and restates your thesis statement.

Step 4: Write a rough draft

Drafting can only be stated on the basis of a perfect outline.

- Write your body paragraphs. Starting by writing the main points and focusing on supporting your thesis.
- Write the conclusion. Start by briefly restating the thesis statement, then remind the reader of the points you covered over the course of the paper. Slowly zoom out of the topic as you write, ending on a broad note by emphasizing the larger implication of your findings.
- Write the introduction. The introduction is, in many respects, the conclusion written in reverse: start by generally introducing the larger topic, then orient the reader in the area you've focused on, and finally, supply the thesis statement.
- Document your paper.

Step 5: Edit and refine your paper

Have at least one, but preferably two or more people look over your essay. Have them edit for basic grammatical and spelling errors as well as the persuasiveness of your essay and the flow and form of your paper.

Step 6: Create the final draft.

Go through your paper and fix all mistakes, rearranging information if necessary. Adjust the font, line spacing, and margins to meet the requirements set by your professor or profession.

3. Styles of professional papers writing

(1) Features of academic writing

- Complexity

Written language is lexically denser: more noun-based phrases, more nominalizations, and more lexical variation.

Written language is grammatically more complex: more subordinate clauses, more "that/to" complement clauses, more long sequences of prepositional phrases, more attributive adjectives, and more passives.

- Formality

Academic writing is relatively formal. In general, this means in an essay that you should avoid:

a. Colloquial words and expressions; "stuff", "a lot of", "thing", etc.

b. Abbreviated forms: "can't", "doesn't", "shouldn't".

c. Two-word verbs: "put off", "bring up".

d. Sub-headings, numbering and bullet-points in formal essays.

- Objectivity

Written language is in general objective rather than personal. Therefore, avoid words like "I", "me", "myself".

e. g. Don't write: "In my opinion, this a very interesting study."

Write: "This is a very interesting study."

Don't write: "You can easily forget how different life was 50 years ago."

Write: "It is easy to forget how difficult life was 50 years ago."

- Explicitness

Academic writing is explicit in its signposting of the organization of the ideas in the text. These connections can be made explicit by the use of different signaling words. Academic writing is explicit in its acknowledgment of the sources of the ideas in the text.

- Hedging

An important feature of academic writing is the concept of cautious language, often called "hedging" or "vague language".

Language used in Hedging:

Introductory verbs: e.g. seem, tend, appear

Certain lexical verbs: e.g. assume, suggest

Certain modal verbs: e.g. will, must, would

Adverbs of frequency: e.g. often, sometimes

Modal adverbs: e.g. certainly, definitely

Modal adjectives: e.g. certain, definite, clear, probable

Modal nouns: e.g. assumption, possibility

That clauses: e.g. It could be the case that…

To-clause + adjective: e.g. It may be possible to obtain….

(2) Reducing informality in academic writing

Language in academic writing is usually described as formal, concise, precise, and neutral. If these characteristics fail to appear in writing, even the most innovative and intelligent ideas might be perceived as simplistic or even be disregarded by a scholarly community. To avoid this situation, writers should strive for formality in their writings. This part outlines language features that usually contribute to informality and provides examples of more formal alternatives.

Note: It is crucial to remember that the language features described below and NOT completely avoided in all academic writing. Depending on the context, discipline, genre, year of publication, and even section of a paper, these features could appear with varying frequency. Still, they are generally uncommon in academic writing (Tab. 3.1).

Tab. 3.1 Informal Features and Possible Substitutions

	Informal Features	Possible Substitution
It is uncommon to address the reader in academic writing. Avoid second person pron. (you/your/yours)	**You** will find the results in Figure 2.	Results can be found in Figure 2.
Contractions (e.g. don't, he'd, she's) make writing less formal. Use full forms instead	The study **doesn't** examine…	The study **does not** examine …
Generally, questions are not used in scholarly writing (unless it is a research question).	**Why** has antibiotic resistance increased?	Many studies have investigated why antibiotic resistance has increased.
Avoid exclamations	… evidence!	… evidence.
Use 1-word verbs instead of 2-or more word verbs (phrase verbs).	This article **talks about** … The prices **go up** …	This article **discusses** … The prices **increase** …

Unit 3 Academic Paper Writing

Continue Tab. 3.1

	Informal Features	Possible Substitution
Avoid unattended this/these; use this/these + a summary word instead.	Writing instructors know that students need to understand the differences between formal and informal language. **This** can help students make strategic choices in their writing.	Writing instructors know that students need to understand the differences between formal and informal language. **This understanding** can help students make strategic choices in their writing.
Limit the use of "run on" expressions, such as: and so on; etc.	Examples include laptops, smart phones, **etc.**	Examples include laptops, smart phones, and other devices.
Single-word negatives are more formal.	Not many of the participants saw a change. This study did not show any contradictory findings.	Few participants saw a change. The study showed no contradictory findings.
"There is" and "There are" can usually be cut from the beginning of sentences.	There was little evidence…	Little evidence appeared …
Limit the use of coordinating conjunctions (for, and, nor, but, or, yet, so) at the beginning of sentences.	And the study also compared …	The study also compared …
Do not use first person (I/me/mine or we/our/ours), or use it sparingly. Avoid first person pronouns unless they are used frequently in your field, in a specific writing genre (e.g. personal reflection) or in a certain part of a paper (e.g. in introductions to state the purpose of research).	I can explain this fact by …	This fact can be explained by …

· 51 ·

Word Choice

In addition to the language features listed above, it is important to be mindful of general word choice as well. The following verbs, nouns, adjectives, and adverbs might be too general or vague, so usually, more specific alternatives are preferred (Tab. 3.2).

Tab. 3.2 Informal Words and Possible Substitutions

	Informal Words	Possible Substitutions
Verbs	get	collect, gain
	make	produce, construct
	put	place, locate
	let	allow, permit
	look	appear, seem
	say	discuss, explain, suggest
Nouns	Thing(s), stuff	use a word more specific to the context
	Kids	child, children, sons, daughter(s)
	people	experts, students, participants, or any other specific words
Adjectives & Adverbs	sort of	rather, somewhat
	like	such as, for example
	very/really/so	omit and use a stronger adjective/ adverb
	lots/ a lot of	a great number /amount of, a variety of
	big	substantial, significant
	bad	negative, unhealthy
	good	positive, considerable, high-quality
	done	finished, completed
	nice	personable, helpful
	beautiful	

4. Format of a Scientific Paper

The scientific format may seem confusing for the beginning science writer due to its rigid structure which is so different from writing in the humanities. One reason for using this format is that it is a means of efficiently communicating scientific findings to the broad community of scientists in a uniform manner.

Unit 3 Academic Paper Writing

Another reason, perhaps more important than the first, is that this format allows the paper to be read at several different levels. For example, many people skim titles to find out what information is available on a subject. Others may read only titles and abstracts. Those wanting to go deeper may look at the tables and figures in the results, and so on. The take-home point here is that the scientific format helps to ensure that at whatever level a person reads your paper (beyond title skimming), they will likely get the key results and conclusions.

Most journal-style scientific papers are subdivided into the following:

Title,
Author's name and Affiliation,
Abstract,
Keywords,
Body,
Acknowledgements,
Reference.

And in the body of a scientific paper, we may include

Introduction,
Materials and Methods,
Results,
Discussion,
Conclusion.

Task 2: Title

⏳ General Knowledge

The most important component of any textual document is its title and it bears great importance which is why a wrong headline choice can make or break the quality of the paper you submit. Why?

- The title is indicative of the subject matter;
- It may influence, to a certain degree, the decision as to whether the research paper will be read, accepted and published;

The title must be descriptive and tell only what the article is about —neither why you wrote is, what you found, nor the conclusion you reached.

According to Zeiger (1991: 305), the hallmarks of a good title are that:

- It accurately, completely, and specifically identifies the main topic or the main point of the paper;
- Is unambiguous;
- Is concise;
- Begins with an important term.

From a syntactic point of view, a title "is metadata with a structure that can be a word, phrase, expression, or sentence, that serves to indicate a paper or one of its parts and give its subject". Consequently, a good title should provide reasonable answers to the following two questions:

- Does the title of your manuscript, seen in isolation, give a full yet concise and specific indication of the work reported?
- Would someone interested in the exact topic of your paper, reading this title, be inclined to read the abstract?

Writing a research paper title may seem a simple task, but it requires some serious thought. Readers come across research paper titles in searches through databases and reference sections of research papers. They deduce what a paper is about and its relevance to them based on the title. Considering this, it is clear that the title of your paper is the most important determinant of how many people will read it.

A Good Research Paper Title

Condenses the paper's content in a few words

Captures the readers' attention

Differentiates the paper from other papers of the same subject area

A good title should include the following three elements:
- The name of the organism studied;
- The particular aspect or system studied;
- The variables manipulated.

e. g.

Processing of X-ray Diffraction Data Collected in Oscillation Mode

The Steps to Create Good Titles

Follow these steps....

1. Answer some basic questions about your paper

- What is my paper about?
- What methods/techniques did I use to perform my study?
- What or who was the subject of my study?
- What were the results?

For example:
- What is my paper about?

—*My paper studies how program volume affects outcomes for liver transplant patients on the waiting list.*

- What methods/techniques did I use to perform my study?

—*I employed a case study.*

- What or who was the subject of my study?

—*I studied 60 liver transplant patients on a waiting list in the US aged 20-50 years.*

- What were the results?

—*Positive correlation between waiting list volume and poor outcome of the transplant procedure.*

2. Identify and list keywords and phrases

From the above answers, we can identify the keywords and phrases as follows:

*My paper studies how **program volume** affects **outcomes** for **liver transplant patients** on the **waiting list**.*

*I employed a **case study**.*

*I studied **60 liver transplant patients** on a waiting list in the **US aged 20-50** years.*

The results indicate a positive correlation** between waiting list volume and poor outcome of **transplant procedure.

3. Write one long sentence with these keywords

Using the keywords and phrases identified in the last step, we can create one long sentence as follows:

This study used a case study of 60 liver transplant patients around the US aged 20-50 years to assess how the waiting list volume affects the outcome of liver transplantation in patients, results indicate a positive correlation between increased waiting list volume and a negative prognosis after the transplant procedure.

This sentence is obviously too long for a title, so we will trim and polish is in the next two steps.

4. Create a working title

Delete unnecessary and redundant words.

Keep all of the most important information.

A case study of 60 liver transplant patients around the US aged 20-50 years to assess how waiting list volume affects outcome of transplantation positive correlation between increased waiting list volume and a negative prognosis.

Then shift some words around and rephrase it to make it sound more natural and shorter.

A case study of 60 liver transplant patients around the US aged 20-50 years assessing the impact of waiting list volume on the outcome of transplantation and showing a positive correlation between increased waiting list volume and negative prognosis. (38 Words)

This is getting closer to what we want in a title, which is just the most important information. But the word count for this working title is still 38 words, whereas the averaged published journal article is much fewer. Therefore, we need to delete the some words and phrases which are not essential to this title in the next step.

5. Delete all extra words and phrases; put keywords at beginning and end

In the working title we created in the last step, the number of patients studied and the exact outcome are not the most essential parts of the paper, so remove those elements first. Then remove the methods used in the study which are not usually the most searched-for keywords in databases. Then we can get the following title:

Assessing the impact of waiting list volume on outcome and prognosis in liver transplantation patients. (15 words)

In the above final version of the title, we can easily recognize the subject and the objectives of the study. Meanwhile, "Assessing", which is the main action of the study, is put at the beginning; and "liver transplantation patients", the specific subject of the study, is placed at the end. This will be very helpful in search engine and database queries.

Tips for Writing the Title

1. Present tense

Titles are always in the present tense. Not too general:
Trends in living alone among elderly Chinese

2. Nor too detailed

Figures for living alone among 3,000 men and women aged over 65 years in Northern China from 1950 to 2000 rise from 17 to 37%

3. Front-focus

Showing front focus, the versions below are even better:
Living alone among those over 65 in southern Finland: a comparative demographic population-based study of trends, 1950- 2000 (descriptive)
OR

Increased solitary living among the elderly of southern Finland, 1950- 2000: A population-based study (more declarative, based on its first word)

These are professional, and the colon (:) is popular. We have reduced this from 25 to 14 words and moved the focus forward. To be very concise, we could reduce it to 12 or even to 8 words.

Living alone among Finland's elderly: Trends toward an increase, 1950 to 2000

OR

The elderly in Finland: solitary living, 1950-2000

4. Avoid articles, except "the" for unique items

Avoid articles in titles, except "the" for unique items (the "only/usual/best /elderly X").

5. Avoid sentence-titles

To avoid sentence-titles, change temporal verbs into participles, or even into infinitives.

X Leads to becomes X, leading to or X, found to lead to ….

6. No abbreviations and jargon

No abbreviations in titles, unless it is pH, DNA or AIDS. Write out each term in the title. And jargon that would not be immediately familiar to the readers should be left out.

Note: Titles with only their first word capitalized are more British; Titles with their main words capitalized are more USA.

Task 3: Abstract

Format of Writing an Abstract

The format of your abstract will depend on the work being abstracted. When preparing to draft your abstract, keep the following key process elements in mind:

- **Introduction/Problem statement**

Why was the study undertaken? What was the research question, the tested hypothesis or the purpose of the research?

- **Methods**

When, where, and how was the study done? What materials were used or who was included in the study groups?

- **Results**

What answer was found to the research question; what did the study find? Was the tested hypothesis true?

- **Conclusion/implications**

What might the answer imply and why does it matter? How does it fit in with what other researchers have found? What are the perspectives for future research?

General knowledge

What is abstract?

An abstract is a 150- to 250-word paragraph that provides readers with a quick overview of your essay or report and its organization. It should express your thesis (or central idea) and your key points; it should also suggest any implications or applications of the research you discuss in the paper.

According to Carole Slade, an abstract is "a concise summary of the entire paper".

- The function of an abstract is to describe, not to evaluate or defend, the paper.

- The abstract should begin with a brief but precise statement of the problem or issue, followed by a description of the research method and design, the major findings, and the conclusions reached.

- The abstract should contain the most important keywords referring to method and content: these facilitate access to the abstract by computer search and enable a reader to decide whether to read the entire dissertation.

Note: Your abstract should read like an overview of your paper, not a proposal for what you intended to study or accomplish. Avoid beginning your sentences with phrases like, "This essay will examine..." or "In this research paper I will attempt to prove..."

Types of Abstracts

There are two types of abstracts: **descriptive/indicative** and **informative**. They have different aims, so as a consequence they have different components and styles.

A descriptive abstract indicates the type of information found in the work. It makes no judgments about the work, nor does it provide results or conclusions of the research. It does incorporate keywords found in the text and may include the purpose, methods, and scope of the research.

Descriptive abstracts are generally used for humanities and social science papers or psychology essays. This type of abstract is usually very short (50-100 words). Most descriptive abstracts have certain key parts in common. It Includes:

- Purpose of the work(objectives)
- Method used
- Scope of the work

Doesn't include:

- Results, conclusions, and recommendations

The majority of abstracts are **informative**. While they still do not critique or evaluate a work, they do more than describe it. A good informative abstract acts as a surrogate for the work itself. That is, the writer presents and explains all the main arguments and the important results and evidence in the complete article/paper/book. An informative abstract includes:

- Problem statements, objectives, and the scope of the work
- Methods or processes
- Results
- Conclusions or recommendations

To be brief, informative abstract answers these questions in about 100 -250 words:

- Why did you do this study or project?
- What did you do, and how?
- What did you find?
- What do your findings mean?

If the paper is about a new method or apparatus, the last two questions might be changed to:

What are the advantages (of the method or apparatus)?

How well does it work?

So when preparing to draft your abstract, ask yourself the following questions:

Reason for writing	Why is the research important?
Problem	What is the work trying to answer? What are the main arguments, claim, and thesis?
Methodology	How was the research performed? Scientific abstracts may include specific research models or approaches used in the larger study. Other abstracts, including literary, may describe the types of evidence used in the research.
Results	What outcomes must be reported? Scientific work may indicate specific results of the project. Other abstracts may discuss findings in a more general way.
Implications	What changes should be implemented as a result of the findings? How does this work add to the body of knowledge on the topic?

Sample Demonstration

Abstract from an engineering scientific report

(S1)A detailed comparison of the properties of the research and microstructures of conventionally sintered and microwave sintered samples of 3 mol% and 8 mol% yttria zirconia was performed. (S2) Identical thermal profiles were used for both types of heating. (S3)For both materials, microwave heating was found to enhance the densification processes which occur during constant rate heating. (S4)The 3 mol% yttria zirconia material exhibited a shift in the grain sizes at densities below 96% of theoretical density, and at higher densities, significant grain growth occurs; while for the 8 mol% yttria zirconia material, the grain size/density relationship remained unchanged. (S5)Differences in the response of the two materials are attributed to the differences in the activation energy for grain growth, and in grain boundary mobility. (S6)Modulus of rupture and toughness of both microwave and conventionally sintered samples were similar. (S7)Following isothermal heating at 13,000 ℃, microwave heated samples were found to be significantly more dense than conventionally heated samples. (S8)This temperature also restricted grain growth once densification was approaching completion. (S9)These findings have significant implications for the commercial application of microwave sintering. (S10)It appears that this method of sintering produces a superior product to conventional sintering.

Analysis:

The above example clearly illustrates how to answer the questions in a well-composed abstract. At the very beginning, it summarizes to one sentence to answer the question "What is the work trying to answer?" And again, explain, in one sentence, "how you tackled the research question", that is, the method you take in your experiment. (S2) In the following sentences(S3-S8), explore the results of the experiment. S3 is the summary of the overall results, and the followings are the detailed results for the two experiment's samples(S4-S5). In S6 and S7, it explains the further results, making a comparison of the methods of sintering. Finally, the last two sentences summarize the conclusion of the experiment and the significance of the research.

Sections of an Abstract:

Although some journals still publish abstracts that are written as free-flowing paragraphs, most journals require abstracts to conform to a formal structure within a word count of, usually, 200–250 words. The usual sections defined in a structured abstract are the **Problems Statement, Methods, Results, and Conclusions**; other headings with similar meanings may be used (eg, Introduction in place of Background or Findings in place of Results). Some journals include additional sections, such as Objectives (between Background and Methods) and Limitations (at the end of the abstract). In the rest of this paper, issues related to the contents of each section will be examined in turn.

1. Problems statement

This section should be the shortest part of the abstract and should very briefly outline the following information:

- What is already known about the subject, related to the paper in question
- What the study intended to examine (or what the paper seeks to present)

In most cases, the Problem Statement can be framed in just 1-2 sentences, with each sentence describing a different aspect of the information referred to above; sometimes, even a single sentence may suffice. The purpose of the Problem Statement is to provide the reader with a background to the study, and hence to smoothly lead into a description of the methods employed in the investigation.

2. Methods

The methods section is usually the second-longest section in the abstract. It should contain enough information to enable the reader to understand what was done, and how.

Carelessly written methods sections lack information about important issues such as sample size, numbers of patients in different groups, doses of medications, and duration of the study. Readers have only to flip through the pages of a randomly selected journal to realize how common such carelessness is.

3. Results

The results section is the most important part of the abstract and nothing should compromise its range and quality. This is because readers who peruse an abstract do so to learn about the findings of the study. The results section should, therefore, be the longest part of the abstract and should contain as much detail about the findings as the journal word count permits.

4. Conclusions

This section should contain the most important take-home message of the study, expressed in a few precisely worded sentences. Usually, the finding highlighted here relates to the primary outcome measure; however, other important or unexpected findings should also be mentioned. It is also customary, but not essential, for the authors to express an opinion about the theoretical or practical implications of the findings, or the importance of their findings for the field. Thus, the conclusions may contain three elements:

- The primary take-home message
- The additional findings of importance
- The perspective

Despite its necessary brevity, this section has the most impact on the average reader because readers generally trust authors and take their assertions at face value. For this reason, the conclusions should also be scrupulously honest; and authors should not claim more than their data demonstrate.

Sample Demonstration

Sample 1: Descriptive Abstract

Role of Pathway in Self-Access Centers

Abstract

This article discusses some roles for self-access pathways, particularly in cultures which have no tradition of self-study. It suggests how pathways might influence the design and running of self-access centers, and gives an illustration of how pathways were designed and employed in a center in China. Feedback is based on mini-survey distributed to thirty users.

Sample 2: Informative Abstract

Sample of IMRaD abstract

This paper analyzes how novices and experts can safely adapt and transfer their skills to new technology in the medical domain.	→ Purpose
To answer this question, we compared the performance of 12 novices (medical students) with the performance of 12 laparoscopic surgeons (using a 2D view) and 4 robotic surgeons, using a new robotic system that allows a 2D and 3D view. Our results showed a trivial effect of expertise (surgeons generally performed better than novices). Results also revealed that experts have adaptive transfer capacities and are able to transfer their skills independently of the human-machine system. However, the expert's performance may be disturbed by changes in their usual environment. From a safety perspective, this study emphasizes the need to take into account the impact of these environmental changes along with the expert's adaptive capacities.	→ Method →Results →Implication

Note: ***IMRAD*** *or* ***IMRaD*** *(Introduction, Methods, Results, and Discussion) is a common organizational structure (a document format) in scientific writing. IMRaD is the most prominent norm for the structure of a scientific journal article of the original research type.*

⧗ Check Your Understanding:

Answer the following questions as briefly as possible:

(1) What is the purpose of the research?
(2) What model was used in the research?
(3) What are the results of the research?
(4) What do the results imply?

Tips for Writing an Abstract

Because the abstract provides the highlights of the paper, you should draft your abstract after you have written a full draft of the paper. Doing so, you can summarize what you've already written in the paper as you compose the abstract.

● Abstracts must include sufficient information for reviewers to judge the nature and significance of the topic, the adequacy of the investigative strategy, the nature of the results, and the conclusions. The abstract should summarize the substantive results of the work and not merely list topics to be discussed.

● Abstracts highlight major points of your research and explain why your work is important; what your purpose was, how you went about your project, what you learned, and what you concluded.

● Remember to use keywords important to your field of research or to use words that indicate your field (biochemical engineering, for example, or the history of Byzantine art).

● Your abstract should not be so detailed that it requires quotations, citations, or footnotes. Remember, it's a summary!

● Avoid using "I" or "we", and choose active verbs instead of passive when possible (the study tested rather than it was tested by the study).

● If possible, avoid trade names, acronyms, abbreviations, or symbols. You would need to explain them, and that takes too much room.

Useful Expressions and Sentence Patterns

1. Problem statement

常用动词：present, summarize, review, outline, argue, account for, address, characterize, concern, contribute, describe, disclose, deal with, devote to, explain, introduce, present, report

句式：

(1) An all-metal CO_2 laser （全金属二氧化碳激光器）is presented in this paper.

(2) This paper reviews/presents the mathematical model and its algorithm used for …

(3) The calibration and experiment design of multivariate force sensors are discussed.

(4) The principles and methodology of language teaching are described in this article.

(5) The long-term performance of various systems was determined, and the economic parts of solar hot water production were investigated in this work.

2. Purposes

常用词：

名词：purpose, aim, objective, goal

动词：aim, attempt to, initiate, intend to, seek

句式：

(1) The purpose /main objective of this study is to explore new methods on/of/for …

(2) The paper attempt to define …in terms of…

(3) Based on recent research, the author intends to outline the framework of…

(4) The study is aimed at finding out the basic similarities between Chinese and Western personality structure and the availability of western personality scales to be used in measuring Chinese.

3. Processes and scope

常用词

过程：analyze, consider, discuss, examine, study, investigate, state, propose

范围：contain, cover, include, outline, scope, field, domain

句式：

(1) The characteristic of …was investigated.

(2) We study the one-step-synthesis method for … in this paper.

(3) The principle of constructing … is proposed

(4) This study identifies /states /outlines the procedures for …

(5) The scope of the study covers…

4. Experimental processes

常用词：

experiment, test, sample

句式：

(1) The samples of pyroelectric ceramics（电释热陶瓷）were collected by …

(2) The blood screening test for the AIDS antibody has been carried out on …

(3) We experimented on the sintering property（流延特性）of …

(4) The new protocol architecture for distributed multimedia systems has been tested in …

5. Results and illustration

常用词：

result, cause, increase, lessen, as a result, result in, arrive at, confirm, demonstrate, find, identify, indicate, monitor, note, observe, point out, prove, provide

句式：

(1) It is found/noted that the amorphous silicon nitride（氮化硅）shows a tendency in …

(2) The study of those properties indicates …

(3) The relationship between … and … is characterized by …

(4) The results/ finding of our research show/reveal/indicate that the amount of energy stored in the pebbles depends on the air mass flow rate, the inlet air temperature, and the properties of the storage material.

(5) It was found that the collector inclination angle does not have a significant effect on system performance.

6. Conclusion

常用词：

conclude, summary, to sum up, lead to, in conclusion, conclusion

句式：

(1) It is concluded that the absorption spectra of two kinds of particles include …

(2) On the basis of …, the following conclusion can be drawn …

(3) To sum up, we have revealed …

(4) Our argument proceeds in …

(5) The research has led to the discovery of …

Unit 3　Academic Paper Writing

Task 4: Body of an Academic Paper

Part I　Introduction

An introduction sets up the questions or issues to be resolved or studied. It provides the significant background information for a reader to follow and understand the importance of the topic/study (i.e. why research should be done) and define the limit of the study to direct the readers to a specific focus and make clear its general purpose.

⧖ Composition of an Introduction

Generally, introductions are broken into four moves. However, depending on the discipline, journal, or purpose of the paper, they may be used in different ways. The following are Swale's Moves in Writing an Introduction.

Move 1: Establishing a research field

Describes the current state of knowledge and research on the topic to asserting briefly how significant, relevant, and important your chosen topic is. This usually requires no citation.

　　Eg. (1) Evidence suggests that X is among the most important factors for …

　　　　(2) Existing research recognizes the critical role played by …

　　　　(3) The world's highest incidence of type-1 diabetes occurs in China.

Move 2: Summarize your predecessors' more general research:

Introducing and reviewing items of previous research in the area.

　　Eg. On this question, Smith's 1990 report was the earliest.

Move 3: Establishing a niche

Focus on your own research. In this "however" move, indicate a gap in knowledge to be filled, raise a question where research in field is unclear to answer, and extend prior research to add more information on the topic. Usually, this move is short and can be addressed in just one or several sentences.

　　Eg. (1) Extensive research has shown …

　　　　(2) Smith's analysis does not take into account …

(3) Little is known about the nature of…

(4) It remains unclear why these methods are considered effective.

(5) More research is needed to establish a direct link between X and Y.

Move 4: Occupying the niche

Shows how your research fills the niche and brings new perspectives to the field. It includes: introducing your own research by stating the question you wish to answer, what you hope to discover, what hypothesis you will test, and outlining the structure that the research paper will follow. Novel methods can earn a brief mention, but rarely will an introduction include any results.

Eg. (1) The purpose of this investigation is to explore the relationship between…

(2) This study provides new insights into...

(3) The present research explores, for the first time, the effects of …

(4) This study tests the hypothesis that X is Y.

(5) To discover whether X correlates with Y, we examined … by use of

(6) This paper has been divided into four parts. The first part deals with …

Four Sections of an Introduction

An Introduction mentions general works relevant to yours, showing that you know what has been done in this area. You need not "start with the Romans". Omit facts known to every scientist. Never march over us with a long parade of facts. It generally includes four sections.

1. Open with two or three sentences placing your study subject in context

Example

"Echimyid rodents of the genus Proechimys (spiny rats) often are the most abundant and widespread lowland forest rodents throughout much of their range in the Neotropics (Eisenberg 1989). Recent studies suggested that these rodents play an important role in forest dynamics through their activities as seed predators and dispersers of seeds (Adler and Kestrell 1998; Asquith et al 1997; Forget 1991; Hoch and Adler 1997)." (Lambert and Adler, p. 70)

2. Follow with a description of the problem and its history, including previous research

Literature review answers the question of "What has been done" in the field.
Example
"Despite the ubiquity and abundance of P. semispinosus, only two previous studies have assessed habitat use, with both showing a generalized habitat use. [brief summary of these studies]." (Lambert and Adler, p. 70)

3. Describe how your work addresses a gap in existing knowledge or ability (here's where you'll state why you've undertaken this study)

The statement of the existing problem answers "What has not been done yet".
Example
"No attempt has been made to quantitatively describe microhabitat characteristics with which this species may be associated. Thus, specific structural features of secondary forests that may promote the abundance of spiny rats remain unknown. Such information is essential to understand the role of spiny rats in Neotropical forests, particularly with regard to forest regeneration via interactions with seeds." (Lambert and Adler, p. 71)

4. State what information your article will address

Based on this, the readers' attention is naturally turned to the present study. That is to answer the question of "What am I going to do".
Examples
"We present an analysis of microhabitat use by P. semispinosus in tropical moist forests in central Panama." (Lambert and Adler, p. 71)
"In this report, we summarize our analysis of genomic DNA extracted from lyophilized whole blood." (Torrance, MacLeod & Hache, p. 64)

Tips of Writing an Introduction

Dos
- Consult the Guide to Authors for word limit
- "Set the scene"

- Outline "the problem" and hypotheses
- Ensure that the literature cited is balanced, up to date and relevant (the more relevant, the more space it deserves and the later it appears)
- Define any non-standard abbreviations and jargon

Don'ts
- Write an extensive review of the field
- Cite disproportionately your own work, work of colleagues or work that supports your findings while ignoring contradictory studies or work by competitors
- Describe methods, results or conclusions other than to outline what was done and achieved in the final paragraph
- Overuse terms like "novel" and "for the first time"

Sample Demonstration

Traditionally, electrochemistry is concerned with charge-transfer reactions occurring across a 2-dimensional interface. Indeed, at any macroscopic two-phase boundary, the magnitude, direction and driving force for current density can be described relatively unambiguously. As early as 1933 [1], workers began introducing the concept of a "three-phase boundary" (solid/liquid/gas) in order to allow for direct involvement of gas-phase species at an electrochemical interface. However, since matter cannot pass through a truly one-dimensional interface among three phases, concepts of "interfacial area", "current density", and "overpotential" at a three-phase boundary lack clear definition. For example, where exactly is the current flowing from/to, and what is the local flux density? Also, if we define overpotential in terms of thermodynamic potentials of species outside the interfacial region, what species and region are we talking about? Although the three-phase boundary concept may serve as a useful abstraction of the overall electrode reaction, it does not address these mechanistic questions. Workers studying gas-diffusion electrodes in the mid-1960s recognized the limitations of the three-phase boundary concept [2, 3].	Literature review

As an alternative, they began to break down the electrode reaction into individual steps, some that involve charge-transfer across a two-dimensional interface, and some that involve dissolution and diffusion of molecular species in three dimensions or across a chemical interface. These and subsequent studies have demonstrated that electrodes with i-V characteristics indicative of charge-transfer limitations (e.g. Tafel behavior) can, in fact, be limited by steps that do not themselves involve charge-transfer[4]. Although the solid-state literature has held on to the three-phase boundary concept more tightly than the aqueous or polymer literature, few examples remain today or solid-state electrochemical reactions that are not partially limited by solid-state reaction and diffusion processes.

One example is the O_2-reduction reaction on a mixed-conducting perovskite electrode, which defies rational explanation in terms of interfacial impedance. In order to incorporate non-charge-transfer effects, workers often apply an empirical Butler–Volmer model (for DC characteristics) or an equivalent-circuit model (for AC impedance) that treat non-charge-transfer processes in terms of an effective overpotential/current relationship[5,6]. However, this approach lacks generality and can often be incorrect for treating oxygen absorption and solid-state and gaseous diffusion, which contribute to the impedance in a convoluted manner[7]. Although such models may provide a useful set of parameters to "fit" data accurately, they leave the electrode reaction mechanism only vaguely or empirically defined, and provide little mechanistic insight.

The purpose of this paper is to provide a framework for defining "charge-transfer" and "non-charge-transfer" processes and to illustrate how they are different. We investigate why charge-transfer models have difficulty modeling non-charge-transfer effects, and walk through several examples including the ALS model for oxygen reduction on a porous mixed-conducting oxygen electrode. We then review a recent study of linear AC polarization of $La1-xSrxCoO_3-\sigma$ (钙钛矿氮化物)(LSCO) electrodes on ceria that corroborates the ALS model and demonstrates the importance of O_2 surface

	Existing problems
	The present research: it's purpose and focus

> exchange and diffusion. This study shows that the electrode reaction extends up to 20 microns beyond the electrode/ electrolyte interface, implying that electrode polarization is better described by macroscopic thermodynamic gradients than as an "overpotential".

Check Your Understanding

Answer the following questions according to what you have been informed.

(1) What is the context of the paper?
(2) What field does the present research fall into?
(3) What problem does the research attempt to solve?

Useful Expressions and Sentences

1. Research situation

(1) Sb. tested (developed, reported, carried experiments on, conducted, used …), they found that …

(2) Sth. were (was) conducted (performed, made,…) by sb.

(3) Over the past several decades, numerous studies on the utilization of plant proteins as a partial or complete replacement for fish meal in diets have been conducted using various freshwater and marine fishes.

(4) The previous work on … has indicated that …

(5) Several researchers have theoretically investigated …

(6) There have been a few studies highlighting …

(7) In recent years, there has been an increased awareness of the potential impact of pollutants such as heavy metals.

2. Inadequate studies

(1) Although a number of papers have been published in the general area of …, little work has been carried out for …

(2) Despite the recent progress, there is no generally accepted theory concerning …

(3) … has not yet been thoroughly investigated.

3. Disadvantages of Related Research

(1) However, this method cannot be used to analyze more practical cases in which …

(2) The limitations of … have been recognized. One problem frequently encountered is that …

(3) All of the above models ignored …

(4) The theory cannot apply to other cases of …

4. Studying Contents

(1) This article presents an analysis of examines/is concerned with/deals with/describes and evaluates/concentrates on …

(2) In this paper, we develop some methods for …

(3) The author has limited his studies to the related aspects of …

(4) The problem under discussion is within the scope of …

5. Purpose

(1) The aim/ An important objective/ purpose/goal of the research/ this study / investigation/project/paper/experiment is to find a way for …

(2) This research work has been undertaken to enhance our understanding of the …

(3) On the basis of existing literature data, we carried out studies in an effort to …

6. Structure

(1) The paper is organized into five sections.

(2) This paper begins with a short description of …, and goes on to describe and evaluate ….

(3) Results of experimental testing are provided and discussed … Several conclusions are drawn from the study …

Part II Literature Review

In this section, you will learn how to write a literature review for a research paper.

A literature review is a survey of previous studies related to the present research. It is a concise overview of what has been studied, what has been argued, and what has been established about the topic. It groups related works together and evaluates previous research in regard to how relevant and/or how it relates to the present research. A literature review is written in essay format and is usually organized **chronologically or thematically**. Its purpose is not only to tell the reader the state of scholarship about a given topic, but also to organize and evaluate the major points or arguments of each source.

Specific Purposes of a Literature Review

To narrow down the research problem;
To indicate the perspective of the present research;
To establish the context of the topic or problem;
To seek support for grounded theory;
To gain methodological insights;
To enhance and acquire the subject vocabulary;
To relate ideas and theory to applications;
To review the main methodologies and techniques that have been used;
To provide a framework for relating new findings to previous findings in the discussion section; (Without establishing the state of previous research, it is impossible to establish how the new research advances previous research.)
To make recommendations for further research.

The Literature Review Structure

Most literature reviews can follow the following format:

● **Introduction:** Introduce the topic/problem and the context within which it is found.

● **Body:** Examine past research in the area highlighting methodological and/or theoretical developments, areas of agreement, contentious areas, important studies and so forth. Keep the focus on your area of interest and identify gaps in the research that your research/investigation will attempt to fill. State clearly how your work builds on or responds to earlier work.

● **Conclusion:** Summarize what has emerged from the review of the literature and reiterate conclusions.

Components of the Literature Review

Stage 1: Problem formulation

● To explain the focus and establishes the importance of the subject;

● To discuss what kind of work has been done on the topic;

● To identify any controversies within the field or any recent research which has raised questions about earlier assumptions;

● To provide background or history.

Stage 2: Literature search and data evaluation

● To find materials relevant to the subject being explored;

● To summarize and evaluate the current state of knowledge in the field;

● To note major themes or topics, the most important trends, and any findings about which researchers agree or disagree;

● To determine which literature makes a significant contribution to the understanding of the topic.

Stage 3: Analysis and interpretation

● To summarize all the evidence presented and shows its significance;

● To discuss the findings and conclusion of pertinent literature;

● To provide a summary of your findings from the literature review;

● To explain what your analysis of the material leads you to conclude about the overall state of the literature, what it provides and where it is lacking.

In assessing each piece, consideration should be given to:

- Provenance—What are the author's credentials? Are the author's arguments supported by evidence (e.g. primary historical material, case studies, narratives, statistics, recent scientific findings)?
- Objectivity—Is the author's perspective even-handed or prejudicial? Is contrary data considered or is certain pertinent information ignored to prove the author's point?
- Persuasiveness—Which of the author's theses are most/least convincing?
- Value—Are the author's arguments and conclusions convincing? Does the work ultimately contribute in any significant way to an understanding of the subject?

Common Ways to Organize Information in a Literature Review

By Chronological order: starting with the earliest work on the topic and moving through to the latest. Be careful not just to list items; you need to write critically, not just descriptively.

By theoretical perspective: identifying the key theorists and theories that have shaped subsequent writing on the topic.

By methodological type: used when different methodological approaches have clearly presented by issue or theme (thematically): grouping a broad range of loosely associated research into a set of common subject areas (or themes). These themes will form the basis of the different threads that are the focus of your study.

By development of ideas: this could be useful if there are identifiable stages of idea development that can be looked at in turn.

Style

Create a balance between direct quotation (citation) and paraphrasing. Avoid too much direct quoting. The verb tense chosen depends on your emphasis:

- When you are citing a specific author's findings, use the past tense (found, demonstrated);

Unit 3 Academic Paper Writing

● When you are writing about an accepted fact, use the present tense (demonstrates, finds);

● When you are citing several authors or making a general statement, use the present perfect tense (have shown, have found, little research has been done).

Sample Demonstration

Sample 1

Microwave processing of ceramics has been studied as an alternative approach for sintering（烧制）of ceramics because of potential advantages such as rapid heating, lower sintering temperatures, penetrating radiation, more uniform micro structures, and selective heating（局部加热）. However, microwave sintering of ceramics can also be troublesome because of the low thermal conductivity（导热性）and high temperature dependence of the dielectric loss factor（介质损耗因子）of many ceramics of interests. Some of the problems encountered include thermal runaway（损耗）, cracking and the formation of hot spots. Much research has been devoted to learning how to avoid these problems or discover ways to overcome them. In this section, an attempt is made to discuss both experimental and theoretical works that have been performed pertaining to microwave heating of rods and fibers traveling through a microwave applicator. This review will discuss the successes and failures and demonstrate the necessity of continued research on this topic that will be the foundation of this research. **Microwave Cavity Design for Polymeric（聚合体的）Threadlines** Huang developed a resonant microwave cavity for heating of polymeric threadlines. The system was powerd by a 2.5 kW magnetron operating at 2,450 MHz. Thermal runaway was controlled by "utilization of the loading behavior of the magnetron（磁电管）and preselection of impedance mismatch（阻抗失谐）and frequency offset（频率偏置）between the magnetronand the resonant frequency." Huang successfully used the system to heat Nylon monofilament（单纤维）on a laboratory scale.	阐述课题研究的目的和内容 相关问题 文献引述

Additional research is still needed with respect to the previously cited work. Thermal spikes were observed experimentally and verified mathematically. Localized hot spots were also shown and mathematically verified. Johnson et al.[4] calculated a critical temperature for alumina rods, and it was demonstrated that temperatures cannot exceed the critical temperature using microwave energy unless power feedback control or some form of hybrid heating is used. Finally, Vogt et al.[10, 11] successfully heated mullite（多铝红柱石） above critical temperature by controlling the absorbed power and using a traveling wave tube source. This method, however, is not applicable in industrial level processing. The present research entails creating a computational model using heat transfer analysis that will describe microwave heating of moving ceramic rods. This is a first step in designing an applicator that will successfully heat ceramics to sintering temperatures for large scale processing. The model will allow for both axial and radial heat conduction, and mesured temperature-dependent properties are included for higher accuracy. Also, a verification of the critical temperature will be presented, and it will be proved that successful heating can be accomplished by forcing the absorbed power to be constant.	对引述文献的评价 对相关课题研究的比分析与评价

Check Your Understanding

Answer the following questions, according to what you have been informed.

(1) What topic is being addressed in the review?

(2) Whose works are cited to verify the topic?

(3) What's author's evaluation on the literature?

(4) What contribution does the literature make to the understanding of the topic?

(5) What will the author do on this topic?

Mainstreaming Crisis Accommodation Responses to Indigenous Family Violence: Literature Review

The past fifteen years have seen a plethora（过多）of reports concerning the extent of violence associated with indigenous people, with most reports occurring over the last six years since the advent of the Common- wealth programme *Partnerships Against Domestic Violence*. In common with the statistics associated with the Australian community in general, it is recognized that violence concerning indigenous people remains under-reported and that it is therefore difficult to establish reliable data.	课题研究的内容
However, it is also agreed that, despite the difficulties inherent in collecting data of this nature, the statistics that do exist are "sufficient to demonstrate the disproportionate occurrence of violence in the indigenous communities of Australia and the traumatic（创伤的）impact on indigenous people" (Memmott et al 2001:6). In a literature review on *Violence in Indigenous Communities*, Memmott and his team reached the following conclusions… Blagg also reported that indigenous people are significantly over-represented in victimization statistics, and are 4.6 times more likely to be the victims of violent crime than non-indigenous people. Moreover, three-quarters of all these victims are women…. Blagg concluded that "Aboriginal women are in a rare category in being more at risk of violence than their men — criminological（犯罪学的）orthodoxy suggests that males are generally at greater risk of violence than women in a given population" (Blagg 2000:12). Lucashenko has highlighted the problems and dilemmas brought about by an ethnocentric perspective on indigenous violence and its exploitation by some indigenous men… In the Northern Territory, for example, some groups of Aboriginal women "are now saying that they are being subjected to three types of law: 'white man's law, traditional law, and bullshit traditional law'" (Lucashenko 1996: 382-3). … …	相关文献引述

This literature review ultimately raises more questions than it provides answers. Given that the major focus of much of the literature is upon rural and remote indigenous communities where services overall are scarce, it is difficult to extrapolate the findings to urban indigenous people.	对引述文献的评价
Whilst it is evident that indigenous women are using mainstream domestic violence services, the research does not indicate in detail why this may be occurring. The issue of confidentiality had been identified but we do not know to what extent lack of choice plays a major role as well. Nor do we know whether common gender experiences override common racial experiences under certain circumstances.	对相关课题研究问题的分析与讨论

Check Your Understanding

Answer the following questions, according to what you have been informed.

(1) What problem does the author formulate?

(2) Whose works are searched?

(3) What's author's evaluation of the literature?

(4) What are the analytical results from the author?

Useful Expressions and Sentence Patterns

1. Problems statement

(1) Various authors studied ...

(2) Most work was done in the past two decades as a theoretical support for...

(3) Despite books and papers focused on ..., some authors focused on...

(4) These works were followed by numerous other papers, e.g., ...

(5) The past fifteen years have seen a plethora of reports concerning the extent of violence associated with indigenous people, with most reports occurring over the last six years since the advent of the Commonwealth programme *Partnerships Against Domestic Violence*.

(6) Microwave processing of ceramics has been studied as an alternative approach for sintering of ceramics because of potential advantages such as rapid heating, lower sintering temperatures, penetrating radiation, more uniform microstructures, and selective heating.

2. Literature citation

(1) Wong (1998) reported that ...

(2) Huang [2,3] developed a resonant microwave cavity for heating of polymeric threadlines.

(3) Previous experiments have shown that callus cells can produce the same secondary compounds that are produced in whole plants, but the concentrations are often different (Brown and Green 2006).

(4) Lucashenko has highlighted the problems and dilemmas brought about by...

(5) Johnson et al. [4] calculated a critical temperature for alumina rods, and it was demonstrated that temperatures cannot exceed the critical temperature using microwave energy unless power feedback control or some form of hybrid heating is used.

3. Evaluation on literature

(1) ... could possibly be achieved with further study.

(2) Additional research is still needed with respect to the previously cited work.

(3) This method, however, is not applicable in industrial level processing.

(4) Studies into the effects on bone density are unclear.

(5) This literature review ultimately raises more questions than it provides answers.

4. Analysis and interpretation

(1) These results indicate a need for ...

(2) Limited available information seems to suggest that ...

(3) Further research is still required with respect to ...

(4) Also, a verification of the critical temperature will be presented, and it will be proved that successful heating can be accomplished by forcing the absorbed power to be constant.

Part Ⅲ Materials and Methods

In this section, you will describe how you performed your study. This section of a paper provides the methods and procedures used in a research study or experiment. You should provide detailed information on the research design, participants, equipment, materials, variables, and actions taken by the participants. The method section should provide enough information to allow other researchers to duplicate your experiment or study.

The method section should utilize subheading to divide up different subsections. These subsections typically include Participants, Materials, Design, and Procedure. It's helpful to both writer and reader to organize this section chronologically, that is, describe each procedure in the order it was performed, for example, DNA-extraction, purification, amplification, assay, detection, or, study area, study population, sampling technique, variables studied, and analysis method.

Construction

One important section of papers of experimental nature is the experiment description. The description of an experiment is composed of the following elements:

(1) The subjects used (plants, animals, human beings, etc.) and their pre-experiment handling and care, and when and where the study or experiment was carried out;

e.g. We randomly selected 100 children from elementary schools near the University of Arizona.

(2) The materials, measures, equipment, or stimuli used in the experiment, including include testing instruments, technical equipment, books, images, or other materials used in the course of research;

e.g. Two stories from Sullivan's (1994) second-order false belief attribution tasks were used to assess children's understanding of second-order beliefs.

(3) A description of the study site for a field study, including the physical and biological features, and precise location;

e.g. The on-site observatory is composed of six nested catchments on the right bank of the Seine River in Paris, along the axis of the Clichy trunk. The catchments under consideration are densely populated areas with many small retail shops and offices yet very little industrial activity.

(4) The experimental or sample design (e.g. control, treatments, the variables measured, how many samples were collected, etc.);

e.g. The experiment used a 3x2 between-subjects design. The independent variables were age and understanding of second-order beliefs.

(5) The protocol for collecting data and statistical procedures (i.e. how the experimental procedures were carried out, and how the data were analyzed.).

e.g. An examiner interviewed children individually at their school in one session that lasted 20 minutes on average. The examiner explained to each child that he or she would be told two short stories and that some questions would be asked after each story. All sessions were videotaped so the data could later be coded.

Style

The style in this section should be read as if you were verbally describing the conduct of the experiment. You may use the active voice to a certain extent, although this section requires more use of the **third person, passive constructions** than others. Avoid the use of the first person in this section. Remember to use the **past tense** throughout—the work being reported is done, and was performed in the past, not the future. The Methods section *is not* a step-by-step, directive, protocol as you might see in your lab manual.

Sample Demonstration

Sample 1

Experimental apparatus and procedure	
The objective of the present experiment was to investigate the heat transfer characteristics of flowing ice water slurry in a straight pipe, and thus provide fundamental information for the new ice thermal energy storage system.	试验目的

The schematic diagram of the experimental apparatus is shown in Fig.1. The apparatus consisted of a test section, an ice water slurry tank, a hot water circulating loop, and associated measuring instruments. The test section was a horizontal double tube heat exchanger of 2,000 mm in length with an entrance section of 800 mm in length. Ice water slurry flowed in an inside tube of the heat exchanger and hot water circulated in an annular gap between the inside and outside tubes. In this study, two kinds of heat exchanger were used. One was … and the other was….	试验设备
In this study, ice packing factor (IPF=volume of ice volume of ice water slurry) of ice water slurry is a very important factor, so an IPF controller and an IPF measuring device were used. IPF controller, which was a double tube, is shown in Fig. 2…	
For measuring IPF of ice water slurry, the electric conductivity method was chosen in this experiment. It is a method using a principle that… Fig. 3 shows the detail of the IPF measuring device…	测试方法
The experiments were performed using the following procedure. Ice particles were mixed with water in the ice water slurry tank. After controlled IPF and velocity of ice water slurry, it was passed through the test section and heated by hot water. The amount of melting heat transferred from hot water to ice water slurry was calculated with the difference between the inlet and outlet temperature of hot water. In addition, the behavior of the ice particles passed through the test section was recorded by a video camera for flow visualization.	试验步骤
For the present experiment, the ice water slurry velocity, u_i, ranged from 0.15 to 0.6 m/s, the IPF of ice water slurry at the test section inlet, IPF_{in}, between 0 and 15%, the hot water temperature, Th_{in}, between 20 and 30 ℃, and the hot water velocity, u_h=0.35 m/s.	试验条件

⌛ Check Your Understanding

Answer the following questions, according to what you have been informed.

(1) What is the purpose of the experiment?
(2) What did the experimental setup consist of?
(3) Try to describe the procedure of this experiment.

Sample 2

Two groups of international students on a one-year Pre-Masters English for Academic Purposes course, each comprising 50 students, were taught academic writing by different methods and compared afterward. In each group, students were from five different academic departments—Computer Science, Business, Engineering, Life Science and law.	研究对象：人数、来源、条件
The subjects were selected from the second semester—Semester B—of the University of Hertfordshire International Bridging Programme in the 2004—2005 academic year. This program accepts only students from a narrow English Language Proficiency band. Thus, comparable language level among the test subjects was insured.	
The subjects were selected from the 250 students on the International Bridging Programme on the basis of performance at a satisfactory level in the Semester A examination. Students who had performed below the minimum level on the semester A examination were excluded. This criterion was employed to ensure the competent understanding of the tasks and adequate motivation.	
One group (Group A) studied English writing in the traditional way in a class with a teacher. This class met for 2 hours each week in a classroom for 12 weeks and was supplemented with written homework assignments given by the teacher each week. The second group (Group B) met together in a class with a teacher for one hour per week for 12 weeks and were assigned a homework task of spending one hour per week doing exercised from the UEfAP website (Gillett, 2005).	实验过程与实验材料
The test instrument employed in this study was a revised version of the University of Hertfordshire English Language Writing Test (Roberts, 1997), which permits the assessment of academic written language performance. It consists of an academic reading text and comprehension question, followed by a discursive essay on the subject of the reading text.	
Both groups A and B were given the same written examination at the end of the semester. The students took the examination under standard university examination conditions as part of their end of semester examination. The tests were marked using the following categories: task achievement; communicative quality; organization; ideas, content and relevance; and grammar and vocabulary, by two experienced writing examiners and moderated in the standard way to ensure reliability.	统计数据
In this way, it was possible to see the relationship between the students' main academic subjects, and the improvement in their writing ability depending on the teaching method.	

Check Your Understanding

Answer the following questions, according to what you have been informed.

(1) Why does a writer have to include where and when he or she did his or her research?

(2) Why is it necessary to describe the experimental procedures in detail?

Useful Expressions and Sentence Patterns

1. Subjects and participants

(1) Four groups of … were recruited on a volunteer basis.

(2) Three secondary school teachers… volunteered to participate in Study 2.

(3) Ninety… meeting the criteria stated previously were included in the present study.

(4) The participants were 48 people chosen from a sample of …

2. To describe the materials and apparatus

(1) Two sets of compositions for … were used in the experiments. The first set is …, consisting of …and …

(2) The apparatus used for the experimental work consisted of …

(3) The experimental system was based on …

(4) The employed amorphous powder was composed of …

(5) The nozzle（管口材质）is made of …

(6) … was prepared by chemical oxidation of the …

(7) The experimental set-up consisted mainly of …

(8) The … system includes three main components.

(9) The experimental apparatus for … is shown in Fig. 2.

3. To describe methods and procedure

(1) In order to solve the problems described above, this paper applies the theory on …

(2) We present a test method to evaluate …

(3) A novel technique has been employed to demonstrate the …

(4) Four individually labeled spectrophotometer tubes were prepared using different amounts …

(5) We also include the age and the academic status of the individual as explanatory variables.

(6) Here we examine the extent to which previous experience in research collaborations with industry has an impact on engaging in a variety of interactions.

(7) This method allows us to use our survey data to obtain a measure of the breadth of interactions while overcoming the problem of having to aggregate interactions of very different nature.

(8) The experiments were performed under air using the following procedure.

(9) This procedure follows the first four steps of the method proposed by A et al.

4. To describe statistics

(1) We measured the electrical activity of the subject's heart using the electrocardiography procedure described by Alves (1999).

(2) A meta-model approximates the response surface and therefore optimizers use it instead of the simulation model to estimate performance.

(3) Males averaged 12.5 cm taller than females in the AY 1995 pool of English majors.

(4) Overall, 25% of respondents indicated that they had been involved in patenting activities at least once, with Electrical & Electronics Engineering showing the highest percentage (38%) and Mathematics and Computer Science the lowest (4 and 11%), respectively.

(5) The proportion of university researchers surveyed relative to total academic staff as measured by HESA (Higher Education Statistics Agency) is largely similar across UK Regions, ranging from a lowest 12.2% for Northeast to a highest 19.5 for Southwest.

(6) Using the parameters established for inclusion in the data set, data from 93 schools of library and information studies were gathered. A majority of the schools (51%, n=48) appear to offer no course in information literacy instruction.

5. Comparison with other methods

(1) The ... method proposed in this paper differs from others reported in the literature in the following aspects.

(2) The conventional methods described in the previous section are inadequate to generate a ...

(3) In comparison to other methods, this one has the advantage of higher accuracy of ...

(4) A traditional CNC system has a closed structure so that it is difficult to develop new functions. To solve this problem, an open parallel intelligent CNC system is developed for milling.

⌛ Tips for Writing Methods

● **Organize your presentation so your reader will understand the logical flow of the experiment(s); subheadings work well for this purpose.**

Each experiment or procedure should be presented as a unit, even if it was broken up over time. The experimental design and procedure are sometimes most efficiently presented as an integrated unit because otherwise it would be difficult to split them up. In general, provide enough quantitative detail (how much, how long, when, etc.) about your experimental protocol such that other scientists could reproduce your experiments. You should also indicate the statistical procedures used to analyze your results, including the probability level at which you determined significance (usually at 0.05 probability).

● **Describe the organism(s) used in the study.**

This includes giving the:

(1) *source (supplier or where and how the organisms were collected)*,

(2) *typical size (weight, length, etc)*,

(3) *how they were handled, fed, and housed* before the experiment.

● **Describe your experimental design clearly.**

Be sure to include the *hypotheses* you tested, *controls, treatments, variables* measured, how many *replicates* you had, what you actually *measured*, what form the *data* take, etc. When your paper includes more than one experiment, use **subheadings** to help organize your presentation by experiment.

● **Describe the procedures for your study in sufficient detail that other scientists could repeat your work to verify your findings.**

Foremost in your description should be the "quantitative" aspects of your study—the masses, volumes, incubation times, concentrations, etc., that another scientist needs in order to duplicate your experiment.

● **Describe how the data were summarized and analyzed.**

Here you will indicate what types of descriptive statistics were used and which analyses (usually hypothesis tests) were employed to answer each of the questions or hypotheses tested and determine statistical significance.

Part IV Result

In RESULT section, the author should boil down all the facts and data that have been collected. The function of the Results section is to objectively present your key results, without interpretation, in an orderly and logical sequence using both text and illustrative materials (Tables and Figures).

The result section always begins with text, reporting the key results and referring to your figures and tables as you proceed. Summaries of the statistical analyses may appear either in the text (usually parenthetically) or in the relevant Tables or Figures (in the legend or as footnotes to the Table or Figure). The Results section should be organized around Tables and/or Figures that should be sequenced to present your key findings in a logical order. The text of the Result section should be crafted to follow this sequence and highlight the evidence needed to answer the questions/hypotheses you investigated. Important negative results should be reported, too. Authors usually write the text of the results section based upon the sequence of Tables and Figures.

⏳ Style

Write the text of the Results section concisely and objectively. **The passive voice** will be likely dominate here, but use the active voice as much as possible. Use the **past tense**. Avoid repetitive paragraph structures. Do not interpret the data here. The transition into the interpretive language can be a slippery slope. Consider the following two examples:

- This example highlights the trend/difference that the author wants the reader to focus:

The duration of exposure to running water had a pronounced effect on cumulative seed germination percentages (Fig. 2). Seeds exposed to the 2-day treatment had the highest cumulative germination (84%), 1.25 times that of the 12-h or 5-day groups and 4 times that of controls.

- In contrast, this example strays subtly into interpretation by referring to optimality (a conceptual model) and tieing the observed result to that idea:

The results of the germination experiment (Fig. 2) suggest that the optimal time for running-water treatment is 2 days. This group showed the highest cumulative germination (84%), with longer (5 d) or shorter (12 h) exposures producing smaller gains in germination when compared to the control group.

Figures and Tables

Illustrations, including figures and tables, are the most efficient way to present the results. Your data are the "driving force of the paper". Therefore, your illustrations are critical! A good illustration can help the scientist to be heard when speaking, to be read when writing. It can help in the sharing of information with other scientists. It can help to convince granting agencies to fund the research. It can help in the teaching of students. It can help to inform the public of the value of the work. Remember "A figure is worth a thousand words."

The Choice between a Figure or a Table

Tables

Tables can be used to make comparisons of proportions and amounts precisely and easily;

- A table should be self-contained.
- A table is usually placed in a position near its relevant description.
- Provide each table with a number (eg: Table 1, Table 2, etc.) and a title.
- The title should be clear, concise, complete and accurate.
- Sometimes a note is added at the bottom of the table.

Figures

Graphs can be used to compare two variables, and to illustrate correlation and tendency between data directly and effectively; Drawings and Photographs can be used to illustrate organisms, experimental apparatus, models of structures, etc.

Types of figures

Bar charts to compare relative proportions and amounts and show trends and changes over time.

Pie charts illustrate proportions and show changes over time.

Line graphs show trends and changes over time.

Multi-plot charts display correlations between events. Multi-plot charts can be constructed in the following ways: (1) by combining line and vertical bar data; (2) by using a double vertical bar graph, with each bar representing two data sets, one on the bottom and one on top; (3) by using a line chart with individual lines representing each data variable; (4) by using a scatter plot with two distributions.

Samples of tables and figures

Tables are usually three-line table format, aligning to the left for words, to the right for numbers, to the decimal point for non-integrals.

Sample 1 Three-Line Table (Tab. 6.1)

Tab. 6.1 Prices for the three-line break chart displayed in exhibit 6.1

Session	Closing Price	Session	Closing Price
1	135	21	165–
2	132 ↓	22	168 ↑
3	128 ↓	23	171 ↑
4	133–	24	173 ↑
5	130–	25	169–
6	130–	26	177 ↑
7	132–	27	180 ↑
8	134–	28	176–
9	139 ↑	29	170 ↓ ↓
10	137–	30	175–
11	145 ↑	31	179–
12	158 ↑	32	173–
13	147–	33	170–
14	143–	34	170–
15	150–	35	168 ↓
16	149–	36	168 ↓
17	160 ↑	37	171–
18	164 ↑	38	175–
19	167 ↑	39	179 ↑ ↑
20	156 ↓ ↓	40	175–

Legend

↑ —New high: white line drawn.

↓ —New low: black line drawn.

(–)—Price within prior range: no line drawn.

↑ ↑ —White: turnaround line.

↓ ↓ —Black: turnaround line.

Figures should include the following:

- The graphical display
- The annotation: axes, scale, unit, label, arrow, numbers, letters…
- The figure title and legend
- Title first, then a, b, c…in legend
- Do not reiterate the contents of a figure legend in the text
- Figure caption separated from Figure

Sample 2   Pie or Percentage Graphs

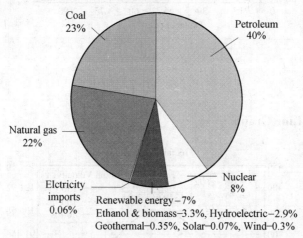

*Totals may not equal sum of components because of rounding

Source: U.S. Energy information administration

Sample 3   Bar Graphs or Histograms

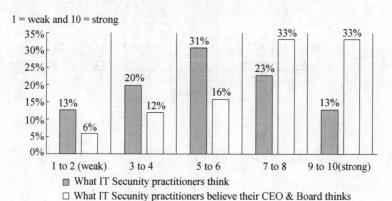

Figure 1. How strong is your organization's security posture?

Histograms

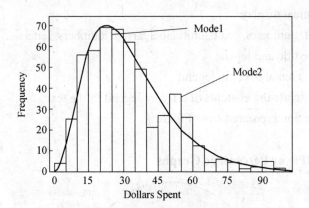

Sample 4 Line Graph

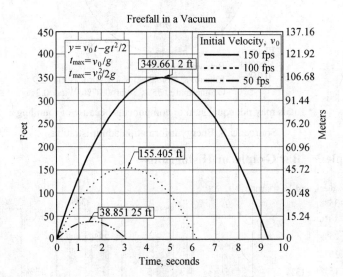

Unit 3 Academic Paper Writing

Sample 5 Scatter Graphs (scatterplot)

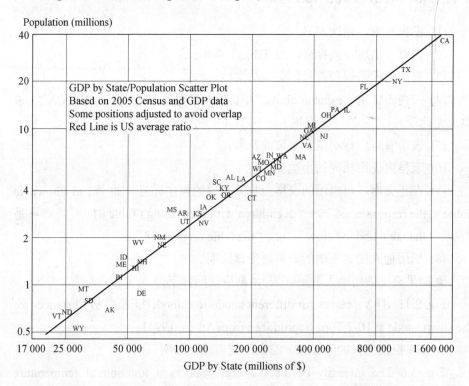

Sample 6 Structure Graph

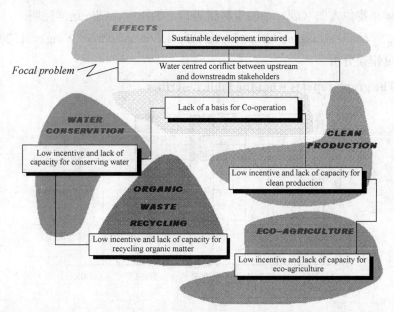

· 97 ·

Tips for Figures and Tables

(1) 根据要求，精选表格；

(2) 表格中出现序列标号，如 Table 1, Table 2；

(3) 表中的缩略词和符号，必须与文中一致；

(4) 表内不宜用"same as above"，要填入具体数字或文字，如"N/A"（未测或无此项）；"—"（未发现）；"0"（实测结果为零）；

(5) 表中参数应标明量和单位的符号；

(6) 表格内使用相同的小数位；

(7) 在正文内，每幅图的表格应按其出现的顺序标号，如"…as shown in Table 8, the responses …"，"…children with pretraining (Table 8)…"，而不是写成"the table above/below"或"the table on page 38"；

(8) 引用他人图、表中的资料时应该注明。

● 如果直接借用他人的图（表），则应注明如下：

Fig. 2.11 Ⅰ-Ⅴ curves for different anode-to cathode(正极负极)distances for the sharp anode at 10-7 Torr. (reproduced from Aiken, 1994)

● 如果根据他人的图（表）绘制，则应这样注明：

Fig. 3.6 The intensity of the 0.2 mm peak as a function of temperature (redrawn from Smith, 2002)

● 如果将他人图（表）中的资料揉进自己的图中，则应这样注明：

Fig. 2.7 analysis diagram on bolt lateral behavior (adapted from Wang et al., 2003)

常见错误分析

1. The graph repeats what the table describes

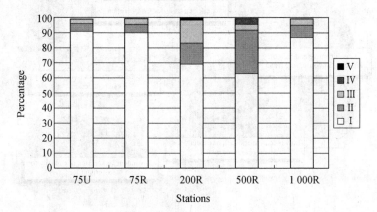

Unit 3 Academic Paper Writing

| | Ecological group | | | | |
Station	I	II	III	IV	V
75U	91.3	5.3	3.2	0.2	0.0
75R	89.8	6.1	3.6	0.5	0.0
200R	69.3	14.2	8.6	6.8	1.1
500R	63.0	29.5	3.4	4.2	0.0
1000R	86.7	8.5	4.5	0.2	0.0

2. Poorly organized figures

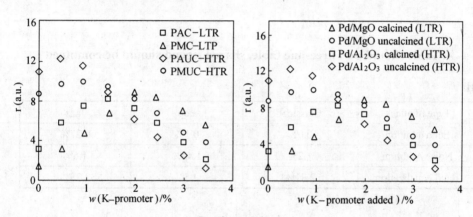

Poorly organized

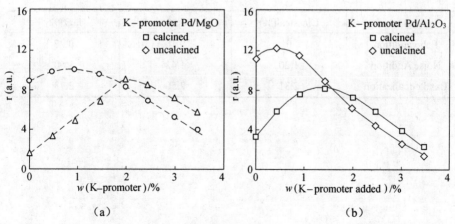

(a)　　　　　　　　　　(b)

Better-organized

3. No figure title, figure legend is unclear

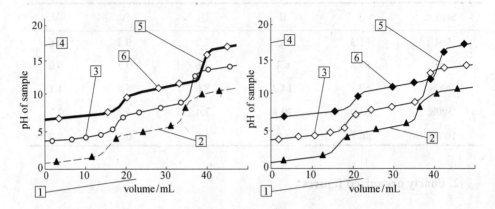

4. Table should be Three-line table, shared legend should be combined

Type of attack	Classical	Pop	Jazz
Echo addition	0.0%	0.1%	0.27%
Noise Addition	1.2%	1.42%	1.6%
Band equalization	2.31%	2.5%	2.73%

Type of attack	Classical(%)	Pop(%)	Jazz(%)
Echo addition	0	0.10	0.27
Noise Addition	1.20	1.42	1.60
Band equalization	2.31	2.50	2.73

5. Materials should be used after selection, the following image too crowded

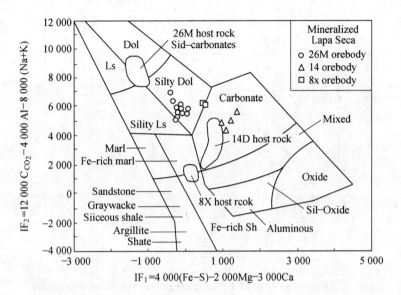

Sample Demonstration

Sample 1

From Figure 7, the tear index increases at first and then decreases as the PET fiber dosage increases. This is because, initially, the binder fibers lead to an increase of the bonding strength of the PPTA fibers and when the PET fiber content reaches a certain point, the bonding fibers form a low tear strength membrane itself. When the PET dosage is 20%, the tear index of the separator is 5.16 mN·m^2·g^{-1}, which is increased by 59% than that of the pure PPTA pulp.

Based on the analysis of the pore size and the mechanical properties, the wet-laid nonwoven material whose PET content is 20% is chosen, as a preference, for the following properties study.

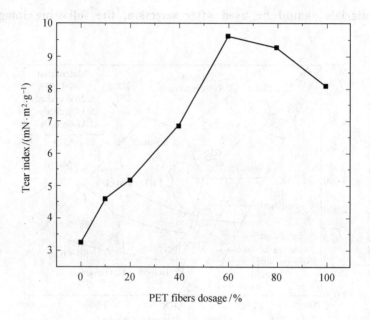

Figure 7. The influence of PET fiber dosage to the tear index of separator

⌛ Check Your Understanding

Answer the following questions according to what you have been informed.

(1) What is the main result in sample one?

(2) What can be implied from the result obtained?

Sample 2

Characterization by XPS

XPS is a powerful technique that allows the detection and determination of the elemental and chemical composition of electrode surface and is an effective tool for the quantification of immobilized or adsorbed proteins. Here, we have used this technique to demonstrate that GOD was immobilized successfully onto WCNT-modified TP electrodes. The surface elemental compositions for TP, TP/MWCNT, and the TP/MWCNT/GOD electrode are summarized in Table 1.

Acting as the substrate electrode, TP consists mainly of carbon (98.58%) and some other minor impurities from its synthesis. It is clear that the oxygen content increased after the deposition of the MWCNTs, which can be ascribed to the introduction of carboxylic groups during the oxidation of the MWCNTs. Concerning the immobilization of GOD, we observed significant increases in N and O as expected from the backbone amide and carboxyl groups of GOD, confirming the presence of GOD. In addition, the flavin adenine dinucleotide (FAD) prosthetic group that functions as the redox center for the electron-transfer process in GOD consists of a riboflavin group bound to the phosphate groups of ADP. Therefore, the appearance of Na and P in the elemental analysis also confirms the presence of GOP. With the increased percentages of N and O, the results from XPS clearly demonstrate that GOP was immobilized successfully on the TP surface, and this conclusion was further confirmed by the FTIR spectra.

Table 1. The atomic composition of TP, TP/MWCNT, and the TP/MWCNT/GOD-electrode surfaces

Electrodes	F 1s /%	O 1s /%	N 1s /%	C 1s /%	Si 2p /%	Na 1s /%	P 2p /%
TP	NA	1.16	0.13	98.58	0.13	NA	NA
TP/MWCNT	1.09	7.96	4.53	86.23	0.19	NA	NA
TP/MWCNT/GOD	2	13.2	6.6	75.2	0.34	1.75	0.92

Check Your Understanding

Answer the following questions according to what you have been informed.

(1) What is the main result from Table 1?

(2) What can be implied from the result obtained?

Sample 3

In the design (as shown in Fig. 5), the sensor of the instrument will be placed into the body of the diesel through the guide door of the diesel, and it can directly scan zones with the most probable existence of stress concentration, such as locations near oil bore and fillet. In case the normal component of magnetic field intensity of the location shows a change from positive to negative or from negative to positive, it means that there may be a tiny crack or stress concentration taking place, and at the same time, the instrument will record in a log and give an alarm. The method is simple, effective and feasible to online testing on operating diesel on ships.

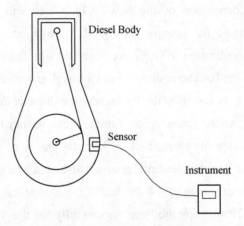

Fig. 5　Diesel Crankshaft Testing Design

Sample 4

Only 34 students, (4% of students who filled in the form and 2% of the total number of registered students), indicated virtual teams as their first choice of study option. Of these, access WebCT from computers off campus but of the students selecting virtual teams as their second choice more than 70% said they would use computers on campus. Of the 25 students who eventually registered as part of a virtual team, 14 had not originally indicated a preference (had not completed the questionnaire) and three others had originally indicated other preferences. This means that of 34 students who originally committed in writing to being in virtual teams, only eight registered as members of such teams. This indicates a high degree of uncertainty or disorganization or inability to find acceptable team members. Six virtual teams were eventually set up, two of which were made up of students who did not previously know each other. Several members of the virtual teams dropped out for undisclosed reasons. In general, these team members never formed bonds or contributed at all beyond initial contacts.

A virtual team is a collection of a small number of interdependent, geographically dispersed, individuals that have a common goal and depend on electronic linking in order to collaborate and achieve it. The teams are often temporary and self-managed.

⌛ Check Your Understanding

Answer the following questions according to what you have been informed.

1. What results can we draw from the description?

2. What can be implied from the fact that so few students eventually register as members of a virtual team?

⌛ Useful Expressions and Sentence Patterns

1. 某个参数或变量在某段时间内的变化情况

参数或变量	一般过去式动词	时间
The enhancement factor	increase	when the applied voltage was from 0 kV to 20 kV.
The pressure	decreased rose fell	after more heat flux was added.
The number of postgraduates in Management School	dropped declined went up went down remained constant remained unchanged	from 1998 to 2000.
The pressure	peaked	after 20 seconds.
The number of postgraduates in Management School	reached a maximum reached a minimum	in 2001.

2. 不同试样、方法或研究对象之间的比较

项目1	用于比较的动词短语	项目2
The power throughput of the condenser	increased much slower than	that of the evaporator.
The NRP algorithm	has much higher packet dropping rate	when compared to the PRP algorithm.
The PRP protocol	has a higher blocking probability	than the NRP algorithm.

3. 不同参数或变量之间的关系或影响

参数或变量 1	关系	参数或变量 2
Pressure	was correlated with was negatively correlated with was dependent on was independent of was determined by was closely related to	the ambient temperature.

4. 说明或评论研究结果

(1) The results suggest that …

(2) These findings are understandable because …

(3) These results agree with Gerner's analysis, in that …

(4) The recognition rate of our system is significantly higher than that reported for Token's system.

(5) The contact angles may have an effect on the time required for the heat pipe to reach steady state.

(6) It appears that heat transfer coefficients are more dependent on heat flux in regions of lower quality.

5. 在对结果提出可能的解释和说明时，可使用一般现在时态的推测动词

主语	一般现在时的推测动词	说　明
It	seems appears is likely is possible	that the Hank visual programming language can avoid some of the syntactic problems associated with textual programming languages.
These results These data	indicate suggest imply	

Tips for Results

Things to consider as you write your results section:

What are the "results"?: When you pose a testable hypothesis that can be answered experimentally, or ask a question that can be answered by collecting samples, you accumulate observations about those organisms or phenomena. Those observations are then analyzed to yield an answer to the question. In general, the answer is the "key result".

Differences, directionality, and magnitude: Report your results so as to provide as much information as possible to the reader about the nature of differences or relationships. For example, if you are testing for differences among groups, and you find a significant difference, *it is not sufficient* to simply report that "groups A and B were significantly different". Report the *direction* of differences (greater, larger, smaller, etc) and the *magnitude* of differences (% difference, how many times, etc.) whenever possible.

The body of the Results section is a text-based presentation of the key findings which includes references to each of the Tables and Figures. The text should guide the reader through your results stressing the key results which provide the answers to the question(s) investigated. A major function of the text is to provide clarifying information. You must refer to each Table and/or Figure individually and in sequence (see numbering sequence), and clearly indicate for the reader the key results that each conveys. Key results depend on your questions, they might include obvious trends, important differences, similarities, correlations, maximums, minimums, etc.

Some problems to avoid:

● **Do not** reiterate each value from a Figure or Table — only the key result or trends that each conveys.

● **Do not** present the same data in both a Table and Figure — this is considered redundant and a waste of space and energy. Decide which format best shows the result and go with it.

- **Do not** report raw data values when they can be summarized as means, percents, etc.

Present the results of your experiment(s) in a sequence that will logically support (or provide evidence against) the hypothesis, or answer the question, stated in the Introduction.

Report *negative* results-they are important! If you did not get the anticipated results, it may mean your hypothesis was incorrect and needs to be reformulated, or perhaps you have stumbled onto something unexpected that warrants further study. Moreover, the *absence* of an effect may be very telling in many situations. In any case, your results may be of importance to others even though they did not support your hypothesis. Do not fall into the trap of thinking that results contrary to what you expected are necessarily "bad data". If you carried out the work well, they are simply your results and need interpretation. Many important discoveries can be traced to "bad data".

Part V Discussion

The function of the discussion is to interpret results in light of what was already known about the subject of the investigation and to explain the new understanding of the problem after taking the results into consideration. The discussion will always connect to the introduction by way of the questions or hypotheses posed and literature cited, but it does not simply repeat or rearrange the introduction. Instead, it tells how the study has moved the readers forward from the end of the introduction.

The primary objective in writing this section is to show the relationship between the facts, their underlying causes, their effects, and their theoretical implications, as well as to explain the facts denoted by symbols or signs of mathematics. To be specific, it includes:

(1) Analyzing the data;

(2) Pointing out the limitations and doubts;

(3) Expressing viewpoints and how the results and interpretations agree/contrast with previously published work;

(4) Stating the theoretical implications and practical application of the study;

(5) Arriving at a conclusion.

Fundamental questions to answer here include:

● Do your results provide answers to your testable hypotheses? If so, how do you interpret your findings?

● Do your findings agree with what others have shown? If not, do they suggest an alternative explanation or perhaps an unforeseen design flaw in your experiment (or theirs)

● Given your conclusions, what is our new understanding of the problem you investigated and outlined in the Introduction?

● If warranted, what would be the next step in your study, e.g., what experiments would you do next?

Style

Use the active voice whenever possible in this section. Watch out for wordy phrases; be concise and make your points clearly. Use of the first person is okay, but too much use of the first person may actually distract the reader from the main points.

Approach

Organize the Discussion to address each of the experiments or studies for which you presented results;

- Discuss each in the same sequence as presented in the Results, providing your interpretation of what they mean in the larger context of the problem.
- Do not waste entire sentences restating your results; if you need to remind the reader of the result to be discussed, use "bridge sentences" that relate the result to the interpretation:

"The slow response of the lead-exposed neurons relative to controls suggests that ...[interpretation]".

Sample Demonstration

Sample 1

The purpose of the study was to investigate whether students in Higher Education on an EAP writing course would benefit from computer assisted instruction.	阐述研究目的
The findings clearly suggested that they do. The students who took part in the computer assisted element of the writing course outperformed those who followed the traditional course in every aspect as shown by their performance on the University of Hertfordshire Writing test.	总结研究结果
They showed particular strengths in the task achievement element of the assessment, suggesting that the computer assisted materials really help the students to understand and focus on the purpose of their writing. It also seems to be the case that the individually directed nature of the on-line materials helps the students to focus on their own	分析研究结果

Unit 3 Academic Paper Writing

specific needs as well as allowing them to access their materials in their own time. Another reason for the success of the materials may be that it allows students to spend more time on the course than is normally the case in a classroom based programme.	
This support and adds the findings of Jones & Smith (1997) and Harris (2002), which showed similar results for an on-line grammar course.	与其他研究相比较
This study has taken a step in the direction of justifying the inclusion of web-based materials in EAP writing course for post-graduate on English language preparation course.	研究的意义
The approach outlined in this study should be replicated with other students in other subject areas, as well as at other levels. In order to be able to recommend the use of on-line materials for all students in all subject areas.	本研究的局限性与未来研究的方向

Check Your Understanding

Answer the following questions according to what you have been informed.

(1) What are the results of the study?

(2) What are the merits of the study?

(3) What limitation does the author point out?

Sample 2

Since the nitrate reduction test was positive, the diesel-degrading bacteria can survive anaerobically in aquifers that have nitrate present.	阐述研究结果
This supports my hypothesis that the diesel-degrading bacterial would be able to grow anaerobically using nitrate as a terminal electron acceptor.	研究结果的意义
If these bacteria were to be used in bioremediation, it would be possible for them to degrade diesel without needing to add O_2 to their environment. Since it is more cost effective to add nitrate to a contaminated aquifer than O_2, and nitrate is more soluble in water than oxygen, nitrate-reducing bacteria have an economical advantage over aerobic bacteria (Htun 2003. Since the diesel-degrading bacteria	分析研究结果

in this experiment are facultative anaerobes, meaning they can grow aerobically and anaerobically, scientists could choose between the two bioremediation methods, finding a balance between cost effectiveness and the time needed to degrade the contaminants.	
Future studies could focus on the effects of additional nutrients on the mineralization rate of aerobic and anaerobic bacteria from Williams Refinery. A comparison could also be done between anaerobic and aerobic toluene-degrading bacteria. In addition, steps could be taken to isolate and identify bacteria present in the diesel-degrading consortium.	未来的展望与建议

Check Your Understanding

Answer the following questions according to what you have been informed.

(1) What are the results of the work?

(2) What are the benefits and drawbacks of the study?

(3) What recommendation does the author make?

Useful Expressions and Sentence Patterns

1. Review the purpose

(1) This research investigated the effects of two different learning methods.

(2) In this study, the effects of two different learning methods were investigated.

(3) We originally assumed that workers who enjoyed a greater degree of privacy would be more satisfied with their jobs.

2. Summarize the most important results

(1) In the first series of trials, the experimental values were all lower than the theoretical predictions.

(2) Our findings are in substantial agreement with those of Smith (1985).

(3) The experimental and theoretical values for the yields agree well.

(4) These results contradict (are consistent with) the original hypothesis.

3. Contributions

(1) The main contribution of the paper is ….

(2) In the longer run, we believe that the ideas presented in this paper may have wider application to such areas of robotics.

(3) It is believed that further research into … will improve the performance of ….

(4) The obtained results may give insight to the thermal systems ….

(5) There are several issues deserving further study.

4. Results

(1) It is possible (may be, is likely) that adding water causes the reaction rate to increase.

(2) These results can be explained by assuming (This inconsistency indicates) that adding water caused the reaction rate to increase

(3) The data reported here suggest (These findings support the hypothesis, our data provide evidence) that the reaction rate may be determined by the a mount of oxygen available.

(4) The reaction rate may be determined by the amount of oxygen available.

5. Limitations and Suggestions

(1) Only two sets of conditions were tested.

(2) The method presented is accurate, but can not be implemented in real-time applications.

(3) Our findings may be only valid for females.

(4) We recognize that a single short test may not fully reflect the subjects' level of competence.

(5) This limitation might be overcome by introducing a …, but this is a subject for future study.

(6) The findings of this study need to be viewed with several limitations in mind.

(7) However, the requirement of … is still a practical limitation. Further research will be devoted to removing this limitation.

6. Application or significance

(1) The results of this study may lead to the development of effective methods for teaching grammar to language immersion students.

(2) Our findings may be useful to educators and others involved in curriculum development.

(3) The technique presented in this paper should be useful in reducing the amount of sludge in wastewater from semiconductor plants.

Tips for Writing Discussion

- **You must relate your work to the findings of other studies—including previous studies you may have done and those of other investigators.**

As stated previously, you may find crucial information in someone else's study that helps you interpret your own data, or perhaps you will be able to reinterpret others' findings in light of yours. In either case, you should discuss the reasons for the similarities and differences between yours and others' findings. Consider how the results of other studies may be combined with yours to derive a new or perhaps better substantiated understanding of the problem. You may also choose to briefly mention further studies you would do to clarify your working hypotheses. Make sure to reference any outside sources as shown in the Introduction section.

- **Do not introduce new results in the Discussion.**

Although you might occasionally include in this section tables and figures which help explain something you are discussing, they must not contain new data (from your study) that should have been presented earlier.

- **Some tips in detail are as follows:**

(1) Make the Discussion correspond to the Results. DO NOT reiterate the results.

(2) DO NOT make "grand statements" that are not supported by the methods or the results Example: "This novel treatment will massively reduce the prevalence of malaria in the third world".

(3) DO NOT introduce new terms not mentioned previously in your paper.

(4) AVOID unspecific expressions such as "higher temperature" or "at a lower rate"; USE quantitative descriptions.

(5) Speculations on possible interpretations are allowed. BUT these should be rooted in fact, rather than imagination.

(6) Compare the published results with your own. BUT DO NOT ignore work in disagreement with yours—confront it and convince the reader that you are correct or better.

Part Ⅵ Conclusion

The function of the conclusion may include: summing up, statement of conclusion, statement of recommendations and graceful termination.

In a paper, any one or any combination of these may be proper. But remember not to duplicate the introduction too much. If the introduction went from general to specific, make the conclusion go from specific general.

It should be informed that some papers do not need a separate conclusive section. Instead, the section of discussion leads to the readers to the end of the paper.

⌛ Sample Demonstration

Sample 1

The Effect of Consumer-Based Brand Equity on Firms' Financial Performance	
In conclusion, the results of this study imply that strong brand equity can cause a significant increase in revenue and a lack of brand equity in hotel firms can damage potential sales flow. That is, if a marketer in hotel firms does not make efforts to improve consumer-based brand equity, then the marketer may expect declining sales and income over time.	总结研究结果
Several implications for future research work are suggested by the findings, some of which are in response to the limitations of this study. First, this study did not investigate every possible extraneous effect that could affect or influence a firm's performance besides brand equity. These may include, for instance, sales promotions, management strategies and innovative activities. Hopefully, future studies will incorporate these variables into their research scope. Second, future research may contrive more realistic and valid measures of financial performance such as ROE, ROS and GROA (gross return on asset). For example, other prevailing hotel performance measure such as yield or market share may be included, in order to more holistically define and predict a form's performance. Finally, future research may develop a more hybrid and composite scale for	研究结果的局限性 对未来的展望与建议

approximating consumer-based brand equity in multiple service industries including hotel brands. In light of these considerations, it is hoped that the findings of this study provide a firm basis on which to undertake additional work.

Check Your Understanding

Answer the following questions according to what you have been informed.

(1) What is the conclusion of the research work?

(2) What are the suggestions for future research?

Sample 2

Conclusion Halfband maximally flat FIR filters have found important applications in the areas of multi-rate systems and wavelet design in recent years. Nevertheless, there has been little work on the interrelation between different families of maximally flat filters, especially those with nonsymmetric impulse response coefficients. In this paper, we have shown that the family of maximally flat filters proposed by Baher is a universal family of maximally flat FIR filters. Specifically, we proved that linear-phase filters of even and odd orders, generalized half-band filters, and fractional delay systems known as Lagrange interpolators all belong to the family of Baher's filters and are obtained by particular choices of three parameters. Besides containing the aforementioned classes of the special filter, Baher's filters are particularly useful because they yield tradeoff between the linearity of phase response and the width of transition band for frequency-selective systems.	研究结果、相关研究的局限性、本文研究的内容、研究结果与结论
A simplified formula has been presented for the transfer function of the filters and its equivalence with Baher's formula has been established. We proved the identity using a modern automatic technique for proving identities that involve binomial coefficients. A computer algebra system was used for automatic generation of the proof. A byproduct of the computer-generated proof is a three-term recurrence relation for the coefficients of the transfer function. The recurrence may find application in variable delay or variable order implementations where the rapid	说明研究方法

update of the coefficients for new values of delay and/or order parameters is a highly desired feature. We have also shown that filters possess an explicit and simple generating function. Generating functions are useful tools that may lead to cellular systolic array structures for digital filters. For a special subclass of Baher's filters, a multilierless array realization consisting of simple double-input cells is possible. A procedure for designing such array structures has been presented.	进一步说明研究结果与结论

Check Your Understanding

Answer the following questions according to what you have been informed.

(1) What are the major results of the research?

(2) What methods were used in the research?

Useful Expressions and Sentence Patterns

1. To make a summary

(1) **We have examined** a very few seconds of sound and **have proposed a small number of** target phonemes for a few bonobo vocalizations. **The methodology, however, is designed for application to a large body of data** – extensive records of discourse interactions between apes and humans, with the goals of …

(2) **This study shows that** the factors influencing the choice of both forms of direct address and terms of reference in a historical material can be measured using present-day theoretical tools.

(3) After these modifications, **it is believed that** the improved beam-type element method is a better method than most others for the analysis of coupled shear/core wall structure.

(4) **We also looked at** the effects of specific error types on students' ability to utilize feedback for editing.

(5) **It was also notable that** the no-feedback control group was more successful in finding and correcting word choice errors than any other error

category.

2. To evaluate the results

(1) The model produced in this study can accurately predict the social and economic impact of road-building on villages in southwest China.

(2) This is good news in that marking errors in this way may be faster and easier for teachers, and more importantly, it reduces the possibility that instructors themselves will make errors while correcting.

(3) Another promising application is to forecast the safety implications of proposed projects by evaluating the levels of safety implied by traffic simulation model outputs.

(4) The findings that students in the no-feedback control group were less successful in self-editing their own text was not terribly surprising and was similar to the result reported by Fathman and Whalley (1990).

3. Future hope and recommendation

(1) Though this study, examining primarily a controlled experimental feedback treatment, obviously has its limits, it nevertheless provides specific evidence that can help teachers weigh some of their feedback options more carefully. Clearly, it also raises further questions for future investigations on this topic. It is to be hoped that researchers will continue to pursue this research agenda for the benefit of teachers and students alike.

(2) Several implications for future research work are suggested by the findings, some of which are in response to the limitations of this study.

(3) In light of these considerations, it is hoped that the findings of this study provide a firm basis on which to undertake additional research work.

Tips for Writing a Conclusion

Conclusions are often the most difficult part of an essay to write, and many writers feel that they have nothing left to say after having written the paper. A writer needs to keep in mind that the conclusion is often what a reader remembers best. Your conclusion should be the best part of your paper.

A conclusion should

stress the importance of the thesis statement, give the essay a sense of completeness, and leave a final impression on the reader.

Suggestions

● Answer the question "So What?" Show your readers why this paper was important. Show them that your paper was meaningful and useful.

● Synthesize, don't summarize.

Don't simply repeat things that were in your paper. They have read it. Show them how the points you made and the support and examples you used were not random, but fit together.

● Redirect your readers.

Give your reader something to think about, perhaps a way to use your paper in the "real" world. If your introduction went from general to specific, make your conclusion go from specific to general.

● Think globally.

Propose a course of action, a solution to an issue, or questions for further study. This can redirect your reader's thought process and help her to apply your info and ideas to her own life or to see the broader implications.

● Create a new meaning.

You don't have to give new information to create a new meaning. By demonstrating how your ideas work together, you can create a new picture. Often the sum of the paper is worth more than its parts.

● Point to broader implications.

For example, if your paper examines the Greensboro sit-ins or another event in the Civil Rights Movement, you could point out its impact on the Civil Rights Movement as a whole. A paper about the style of writer Virginia Woolf could point to her influence on other writers or on later feminists.

Strategies

● Echoing the introduction: Echoing your introduction can be a good strategy if it is meant to bring the reader full-circle. If you begin by describing a scenario, you can end with the same scenario as proof that your essay was helpful in creating a new understanding.

- Challenging the reader: By issuing a challenge to your readers, you are helping them to redirect the information in the paper, and they may apply it to their own lives.

- Looking to the future: Looking to the future can emphasize the importance of your paper or redirect the readers' thought process. It may help them apply the new information to their lives or see things more globally.

Example:

Without well-qualified teachers, schools are little more than buildings and equipment. If higher-paying careers continue to attract the best and the brightest students, there will not only be a shortage of teachers, but the teachers available may not have the best qualifications. Our youth will suffer. And when youth suffers, the future suffers.

- Posing questions: Posing questions, either to your readers or in general, may help your readers gain a new perspective on the topic, which they may not have held before reading your conclusion. It may also bring your main ideas together to create a new meaning.

Task 5: Acknowledgements, References, Notes

Part I Acknowledgements

In academic writing, it is appropriate to acknowledge funding bodies, departments, and individuals who have been of help during the research and writing process. It is advisable to include people in the proper order according to the importance of their assist they paid. So, in your acknowledgement, you can address your supervisor, coordinator, academic crew of your department, support staff, technical personnel of your branch, organizations or institutions, friends and family. In journal articles, the section of acknowledgement is the last part of the section of the body, which may be a brief note indicating gratitude to those who have been of help, whereas acknowledgements in book-length studies (e.g. doctoral dissertation) are usually placed prior to the body of the paper on a separate page. However, no matter where they are located, they all function to express the writers' appreciation. By acknowledgements, the writer:

(1) Start with the most important persons, such as your thesis advisor or major professors overseeing your project, followed by any members of the thesis committee and other supervising academics directly involved in your project.

(2) Lists the individuals, including lab assistants or anyone who helped you with your project or contributed to your project in any way.

(3) Address financial aid you might have received. It would be appropriate to thank the foundation or organization by name if your project received any financial support from them, such as a grant, a fellowship or a scholarship.

(4) Put more personal and emotional supporters last, including your parents, friends, partners or other acquaintances who contributed to your emotional well-being throughout the completion of your project or thesis.

(5) Gives credit to works cited in the text for which permission to reproduce has been granted.

(6) Use the appropriate tone and form. Acknowledgments are always brief and never flowery.

Unit 3 Academic Paper Writing

Sample Demonstration

Sample 1

My work was supported by National Institutes of Health grants CA31798, CA31799, A131921, DK45104, and HL48675. Many references had to be deleted to shorten this review, and I apologize to authors and readers for work that could not be cited. I thank Andrew and Tom Issekutz, Alf Hamann, Eugene Butcher, Mike Brenner, Lan Colditz, Adrienne Brian, Ronen Alon, Doug Ringlet, Mechelle Cart, and Stephen Roth for sharing preprints or unpublished data and David Chang, Chades Mackay, Walter Newman, and Fred Rosen for critical Reviews.

Sample 2

I would like to express my special appreciation and thanks to my supervisor Professor A, you have been a tremendous mentor for me. I would like to thank you for encouraging my research and for allowing me to grow as a research scientist. Your advice on both research as well as on my career have been invaluable. I would also like to thank my committee members, Professor B, Professor C and Professor D for serving as my committee members even at hardship. I also thank you for your brilliant comments and suggestions, thanks to you.

I would especially like to thank E and F for your wonderful collaboration. You supported me greatly and were always willing to help me.

My special appreciation goes to my parents for all of the sacrifices that you've made on my behalf, especially caring for our daughter; to my beloved husband, Dr. G and my sister for your faithful support and encouragement me throughout this experience; to our beloved daughter Joyce for being such a good girl always cheering me up.

Check Your Understanding

Answer the following questions according to what you have been informed.

(1) Whom must an author express thanks to?

(2) How to arrange the names the author wants to acknowledge?

Useful Expressions and Sentence Patterns

(1) I would like to express my special appreciation and thanks to my supervisor, Dr. Smith, for his vital support and assistance.

(2) Thanks to Joe and Black for their friendship in the lab.

(3) This work has been financially supported by A, B, C...to whom I am sincerely grateful.

(4) The work was sponsored by X. Partial support from Y is gratefully appreciated.

(5) I'd like to thank all the faculty, staff members and lab technicians of... Department, whose services turned my thesis a success.

(6) 我国部分科学基金的英文表达

- 中国科学院知识创新项目：Knowledge Innovation Programs of the Chinese Academy of Sciences;

- 中国科学院"十二五"重大项目：Major Programs of the Chinese Academy of Sciences during the 12th Five-year Plan Period;

- 中国科学院重点资助项目：Key Program of the Chinese Academy of Sciences;

- 中国科学院上海分院择优资助项目：Advanced Programs of Shanghai Branch, the Chinese Academy of Sciences;

- 国家教育部博士点基金资助项目：Ph. D. Programs Foundation of Ministry of Education of China;

- "十二五"国家科学技术公关基金资助项目：National Medical Science and Technique Foundation during the 12th Five-Year Plan Period;

- 高等学校骨干教师资助计划：Foundation for University Key Teacher by the Ministry of Education of China;

- 国家杰出青年科学基金：National Science Fund for Distinguished Young Scholars.

Part Ⅱ References/Bibliography

Nearly all research builds on previous research. Researchers show respect to previous work in the field by documenting each source that they use in their papers. If they neglect to refer to someone else's work, then they commit plagiarism, which is regarded as a very serious offense. Referencing systems, vary between different disciplines and different journals or publishers. Despite this variation, all referencing systems have the same basic components: citing sources in the text (i.e. in-text citations), a list of source materials.

Citation of a source is to insert a brief parenthetical acknowledgement in the paper wherever the author incorporate another's words, facts, or ideas. Citations can be divided into two types: direct quotations and indirect quotations. Direct quotations refer to the citation of the exact words from the original source; indirect quotations mean paraphrasing or putting an author's idea or information into one's own words.

A list of source materials appears at the end of the paper with the title corresponding to a specific referencing system, such as "Bibliography", "References" or "Works Cited". As a general rule, a reference list includes only the works that have been cited in the paper; while a bibliography, apart from the above, may also include other books and articles that have been important sources of information in the preparation of the paper.

Here are several widely-used referencing systems:

APA (American Psychology Association): for psychology, education, and other social sciences.

MLA (Modern Language Association): most commonly used to write papers and cite sources within the liberal arts and humanities.

CMS (The Chicago Manual of Style): used with all subjects by books, magazines, newspapers, and other non-scholarly publications.

AMA (American Medical Association): for medicine, health, and biological sciences.

CBE (Council of Biology Editors): used in natural sciences.

MLA and APA styles, both in the alphabetical listing, can cover most fields and here we only take APA style as an example.

Samples

Reference Lists
APA Style for works cited:

The basic form for articles in periodicals

APA style dictates that authors are named last name followed by initials; publication year goes between parentheses, followed by a period. The title of the article is in sentence-case, meaning only the first word and proper nouns in the title are capitalized. The periodical title is run in title case and is followed by the volume number which, with the title, is also italicized or underlined.

Author, A. A., Author, B. B., & Author, C. C. (Year). Title of the article. *Title of Periodical*, volume number (issue number), pages.

(1) Article in Journal Paginated by Volume.

Journals that are paginated by volume begin with page one in issue one, and continue numbering issue two where issue one ended, etc.

Harlow, H. F. (1983). Fundamentals for preparing psychology journal articles. *Journal of Comparative and Physiological Psychology, 55*, 893-896.

(2) Article in a Magazine.

Henry, W. A., III. (1990, April 9). Making the grade in today's schools. *Time*, 135, 28-31.

(3) Article in a Newspaper.

Unlike other periodicals, p. or pp. precedes page numbers for a newspaper reference in APA style. Single pages take p., e.g., p. B2; multiple pages take pp., e.g., pp. B2, B4 or pp. C1, C3-C4.

Schultz, S. (2005, December 28). Calls made to strengthen state energy policies. *The Country Today*, pp. 1A, 2A.

Tips for References

Read GUIDE FOR AUTHORS to study the style of your target journal or the style recommended for the university to ensure the proper format.

Avoid

- Too many references

Prefer reviews and the earliest and best articles. Omit poor, weak papers.

- Excessive self-citations
- Excessive citations of publications from the same region
- Personal communications, unpublished observations and submitted manuscripts not yet accepted
- Citing articles published only in the local language

Part III Notes

Notes have four main uses:

(1) to cite the authority to support statements in the text—specific facts or opinions as well as quotations;

(2) to make cross-references;

(3) to make incidental comments on, to amplify, or to qualify textual discussion—in short, to provide a place for material the writer deems worthwhile without interrupting the flow of thought of the text;

(4) to make acknowledgements.

Notes, then, are of two kinds: reference notes 1 and 2 and content notes 3 and 4. Reference notes may be found within a text (in-text notes), but are more usually presented at the foot of a page (footnotes) or at the end of a chapter or document (endnotes).

Format of Notes

For books:

- Name of author(s)
- Title and subtitle (if any)
- Name of editor, compiler or translator, if any
- Number of the edition, if other than the first edition
- Name of series in which the book appears, if any, with volume number
- Information about publication, e.g. place of publication, name of publishing agency, date of publication
- Page number(s) of the specific citation

For articles:

- Name of the author(s)
- Title
- Name of the periodical or journal
- Volume and issue numbers
- Date and the page number(s)

Unit 3 Academic Paper Writing

General Introduction to Notes

When a note is introduced, whether footnote or endnote, reference or content, it is marked with an Arabic numeral typed slightly above the line (superscript).

General Introduction to Notes

- Never elevate note numbers a full space.

- Don't put a period after a superscript note number or embellish it with parentheses, brackets, or slash marks. The reference note follows punctuation marks except the dash, which it precedes, and goes outside a closing parenthesis.

- Note numbers preceding the footnotes themselves are preferably typed on the line, followed by a period. The first line of the footnote is indented the same amount as paragraph openings in the text.

- The reference note should follow the passage it refers to. If the passage is an exact quotation, the note number comes at the end of it, not after the author's name or at the end of the textual matter introducing the quotation. If possible, a note number should come at the end of a sentence, or at least at the end of a clause.

- Note numbers must follow one another in numerical order, beginning with 1. Numbering starts over at the beginning of each chapter. In papers that are not divided into chapters, the numbers will run continuously throughout. Care must be taken to ensure that the final sequence is correct.

- Double numbers (such as 1,2) should not be used except in scientific fields where this practice is acceptable. Consult an authoritative manual within the discipline for guidelines.

Basic Rules for Notes

1. Footnotes

If only a few notes, in a few words, can serve the purpose in an article or chapter, use the footnote. A footnote may do more than simply refer the reader to another work or page for further information; it may give information on how facts presented in the text were ascertained or confirmed. A footnote usually answers the following questions: (1) Who says it? (2) What is the title of the piece of writing in which he says it? (3) Where or by whom is this writing made available? (4) On what page or pages may the material cited be found? Such a note is useful for conveying supplementary data, as in the following example:

In the United States, by contrast, approximately 49% of psychologists name either teaching or research as their principal activity, compared with only 31% for service functions. Table 15 shows the numbers and proportions of English- and French-speaking[1] Canadians and of American and other foreign respondents in each of the principal work functions. It is estimated that 13%～14% of Canadian psychologists are French-speaking.[2]

---

1. French-speaking Canadians were identified by their request for or return to the French version of the questionnaire. Further identification and response rates were confirmed through follow-up telephone contacts with non-residents.
2. But see discussion by Dr. Belanger on p. 127.

Number your footnotes page by page or chapter by chapter, and thereby avoid the possibility of triple-digit references.

Occasionally two distinct series of footnotes are required: an author's notes and a translator's or editor's notes. Use asterisks and a different typeface for the translator's or editor's notes which should be marked with appropriated abbreviations (trans, or Ed.):

*The "commission" referred to is the Canada Labour Relations Board (Ed.).

Use special symbols or letters to indicate notes within the body of mathematical, statistical and other scientific documents, and particularly with tables and graphs, as illustrated below, since superscript numerals could be confused with mathematical indices:

	1990	1995	2000
Haiti	35	19	2
Canada	1 089	920	3 005

[a] projected   [b] including Quebec

2. Endnotes

Where notes are numerous and lengthy and include extensive comments by the author, use endnotes to facilitate word-processing and cross-referencing and enhance the appearance of the text.

Number your references consecutively throughout the article or chapter, and present the notes in a reference list at the end of the article or chapter.

Notes to Chapter 2

(1) M. Fleming and W. H. Levie, eds., *Instructional Message Design: Principles From the Behavioral and Cognitive Sciences*, 2nd ed. (Englewood Cliffs, NJ: Educational Technology Publications), 1993, pp. 34-35.

(2) Fleming and Levie, p. 66.

(3) B. Joyce, B. Shower, and C. Rolheiser-Bennett, "Staff Development and Student Learning: A Synthesis of Research on Models of Teaching", *Educational Leadership* 45, 2(1987): 11-23.

3. In-text notes

Also known as the author-date notes, in-text notes are usually found in the running text or at the end of a block quotation, and consist of the author's last name, the publication date, volume number or issue number: page number, all enclosed in parentheses. There is no comma between name and date and locate issue number before page number and use a colon to separate them.

For example:

(Wiebe 1993, 27)

(Suzuki 1990, 3:45)

Sample Demonstration

Sample 1

Text with Footnotes

The search for an exact expression of these economic principles naturally led Lotka to the mathematical school of the 19th-century economists represented by

Augustin Cournot, Leon Walras, Hermann Heinrich Gossen, and William Stanley Jevons. [59] These were a school not in the sense of following the same program, but in that they independently explored the use of mathematics in economic analysis. It was to Jevons's *The Theory of Political Economy* that Lotka turned for his principal model, adding a few modifications culled from the early work of Vilfredo Pareto. [60] viewing economics as analogous to the physical sciences dealing with statistics and equilibrium, Jevons tried to develop a program of scientific economics from Bentham's doctrine, creating out of the combination a "calculus of pleasure and pain."[61]

---

59. C. Gide and C. Rist, *A History of Economic Doctrines,* 2nd ed. (London: George C. Harrap, 1048), 599-514.

60. William Stanley Jevons, *The Theory of Political Economy*, 2nd ed. Rev. (London: Macmillan, 1879). Ltka used the 1911 edition, which has the same text. Also Vilfredo Preto, *Mannual of Political Economy,* trans. A.S. Schwier, (New York: Augustus M. Kelley, 1971).

61. Jevons, *Political Economy*, vii.

⌛ Tips for Notes

(1) As you write your first draft, including the introduction, body, and conclusion, add the information or quotations on your note cards to support your ideas.

(2) Use footnotes or endnotes to identify the sources of this information. If you are using footnotes, the note will appear on the same page as the information you are documenting, at the bottom (or "foot") of the page. If you are using endnotes the note will appear together with all other notes on a separate page at the end of your report, just before the bibliography. If you are using parenthetical documentation, you will use the MLA/APA format and a Works Cited page.

(3) There are different formats for footnotes (and endnotes), so be sure to use the one required.

(4) Note that footnotes can be shortened if the source has already been given in full in a previous footnote.

Unit 3　Academic Paper Writing

Task 6: Avoid Errors in Academic Writing

Grammatical and Stylistic Errors

●不完整的句子

(1)（误）Researchers have doubled the previous efficiency of producing hydrogen from water. And have made major advances in carbon nanotube storage technology.

（正）Researchers have doubled the previous efficiency of producing hydrogen from water and have made major advances in carbon nanotube storage technology.

(2)（误）To encourage the use of renewable energy electricity in the United States. Policy measures will be needed.

（正）To encourage the use of renewable energy electricity in the United States, policy measures will be needed.

句子必须表达一个完整概念。它包含比较完整意义的一组词，一般至少包括主语和谓语这两个主要成分。所谓不完整的句子包括：单独孤立的一个从句，两个并列动词谓语分割使用，介词短语、动名词短语、分词短语、动词不定式短语、同位语的孤立使用。

●主谓不一致：

(1)（误）The actual research as well as the company's industrial activities are supported by many skills and disciplines.

（正）The actual research, as well as the company's industrial activities, **is supported** by many skills and disciplines.

(2)（误）The administration building, with its dingy windows and deep gray paint, house the administrative offices, including the infamous "fishbowl".

（正）The administration building, with its dingy windows and deep gray paint, **houses** the administrative offices, including the infamous "fishbowl".

若单数主语后面紧跟 as well as, together with, along with, in addition to 开头的短语，单数主语还是配合单数动词谓语。

分数或百分数+of+名词（代词）结构，谓语动词的单复数形式取决于 of 后名词或代词的单复数形式。

●被动语态的误用

(1) 若使用被动语态来指出自己的行为，一定要清楚表明自己是这个行为的执行者。

(误) Now that the method has been modified, it is used to analyze the chemical heat pump dryer.

(正) Now that we have modified the method, we can use it to analyze the chemical heat pump dryer.

(2) 被动语态的句子所陈述的事情必须与事实相符。

(误) From these data, it is seen that self-phase modulation and the self-frequency shift are enhanced by forward pumping.

(正) From these data, it can be seen that self-phase modulation and the self-frequency shift are enhanced by forward pumping.

(3) 不及物动词不可以使用被动语态。

(误) The calculation was proceeded by the student.

(正) The calculation was performed (carried out) by the student.

●悬垂修饰语的误用

在撰写正式的科技论文时，作者应该特别小心，要避免悬垂修饰语的成分。如：

(1) (误) After connecting this lead to pin1 of the second tube, the other lead is connected to pin2.

(正) After this lead has been connected to pin1 of the second tube, the other lead is connected to pin2.

(2) (误) Comparing Huckin's method with ours, the difference between them is that we don't use external forces to join the panels in the model together.

(正) Unlike Huckin's method, our method does not use external forces to join the panels in the model together.

●不合理的比较

两个项目之间的比较一定要合理且完整，而且两个项目本身是可以比较的相同类型的名词。此外，必须把比较的项目陈述清楚，以免读者不知所云。

(1) (误) The accuracy of the new robot arm is greater than the conventional one.

Unit 3 Academic Paper Writing

　　(正) The accuracy of the new robot arm is greater than that of the conventional one.

　　(正) The new robot arm is more accurate than the conventional one.

(2) (误) These results are consistent with Smith et al. (1998).

　　(正) These results are consistent with those of Smith et al. (1998).

● 词汇不够正式

科技论文趋向于使用正式用语和大词，以突出其正式、清晰、准确的语体特征，而许多中国作者限于词汇量，往往词汇的使用不够正式。

(1) (误) Heat and wetness make micro-organisms multiply.

　　(正) Heat and moisture encourage the multiplication of micro-organisms.

(2) (误) The results obtained fit the experimental values.

　　(正) The results obtained agree with the experimental values.

● 句法不够正式

(1) (误) This signal is too weak.

　　(正) This is too weak a signal.

(2) (误) The energy consumed by this device is less than that by that one.

　　(正) This device consumes less energy than that one.

(3) (误) If the charging-time constant is reduced, both bandwidth and sampling efficiency will be improved.

　　(正) Reduction of the charging-time constant will improve both bandwidth and sampling efficiency.

Word Usage Errors

1. A lot of

A lot of 是口语表达形式，在正式论文中应该避免使用，而应改为 many, much 或 a great deal of 等表达"许多"的意思。

2. Above

Above 可用于指前面提到的资料，不过应以一个段落或前几个句子中曾出现过的资料为限。Above 不能用来说明前几个段落甚至前几页中曾经出现的资料，因为读者会感到迷惑，不清楚 above 所指的资料是什么。

如：The above explanation will help answer this question.

若不是刚刚提及，则应该使用下列写法：

We can adopt the explanation introduced earlier to answer this question.

We can apply the explanation introduced in Section 2 to answer this question.

3. Anymore

在科技论文中，含有 anymore 及否定动词的句子，应该改写成 no longer 与肯定动词组合的句子。

如：The humidifier does not work anymore.

改为：The humidifier no longer works.

　　　The humidifier does not work any longer.

4. Approach

作为及物动词使用时，其后不能紧跟介词 to。

如：When x increased, the value of the function approaches to zero.

改为：When x increased, the value of the function approaches zero.

Approach 做名词使用时，后面常紧跟介词 to 及另一个名词或动名词。

如：Dr. Katern proposed a new approach to solving this problem.

5. As follows

(正) as follows, the following, as shown below

(误) as following, as the followings, as below

如：

Solution for equation (1) and (2) can be derived as follows:

These results in the following expression:

Commonly used methods include the following:

As follows 或 the following 所介绍的内容很少，如一个或数个数学公式，这时后面就需要加冒号。若介绍的东西很长，如很长的例子或者演算方法，就应紧跟句号。

6. As well as

这个并列连词的意思与 and 不完全相同，用 as well as 连接两个并列成分时，重点在前面一项，即其用意在于强调前面的名词。

如：We can turn electric energy into light energy as well as into heat energy.

　　　（我们能把电能转化为热能，也能转化为光能。）

　　　He can operate a grinder as well as a lathe.

（他不仅能开车床，而且也能开磨床。）

7. Aspect

在英文科技论文中，aspect 及 area 之类的词，常常是累赘的，应该加以省略。

如：

累赘：Regarding the application aspect of Genetic Algorithm, many approaches have been proposed.

简洁：Many approaches to application of Genetic Algorithm have been proposed.

累赘：In the area of application of Genetic Algorithm, many approaches have been proposed.

简洁：Many application of Genetic Algorithm have been proposed.

8. Based on

若句首出现以 based on 开头的过去分词短语，则必须注意过去分词表示的被动行为对象是句子中的主语。然而，在绝大多数以 based on 开头的句子中，based on 开头的过去分词短语却不能合理地修饰句子的主语。因此，本着谨慎的原则，最好使用 on the basis of，by, from, according to 或其他词来替代 based on。如：

（误）Based on Eq. (6), it is obtained that …

（正）From Eq. (6), it is obtained that …

（正）Eq. (6) entails that …

9. Because of the fact that 与 because that

这是两个不符合英文文法的用法。如：

（误）Because that no machine ever runs without some friction, overcoming that friction wastes energy.

（正）Because no machine ever runs without some friction, overcoming that friction wastes energy.

（误）This is because that the direct current flows in a wire always in one direction.

（正）This is because the direct current flows in a wore always in one direction.

冗长：Because of the fact that electricity can change into other forms of energy, it is widely used in industry.

简洁：Because electricity can change into other forms of energy, it is widely used in industry.

10. Belong

在英文中，belong 通常表示属某人的财产（后加 to）和应归入某部类（后加 to, among, in, under, with）和适合的意思。但在科技论文中，想要表示某个项目属于某种类型时，通常不使用 belong，改用 to fall into the category of, to be a form of 或 to be classified as。如：

The building belongs to the college.

The problem can be classified as a nonlinear programming problem.

The problem is a type of nonlinear programming problem.

11. Better

在科技论文中，当我们比较两个事物的时候，最好不用 better，而应该使用更精确的词。如：

(模糊) The gas turbine is better than the steam engine.

(精确) The gas turbine is more efficient than the steam engine.

(模糊) Our algorithm is better than the conventional one.

(精确) Our algorithm is faster than the conventional one.

12. Call

call 后面不能加 as，但 refer to 后面必须加 as。如：

(误) They will call this installation as Heat Pump Dryer (HPD).

(正) They will call this installation Heat Pump Dryer (HPD).

(正) They will refer to this installation as Heat Pump Dryer (HPD).

13. Change

若 change 用于描述某物或某现象在一段时间内的变化，则 change 后面的介词应该是 in，而不是 of。如：

(差) The changes of the liquid pressure in the cylinder were measured every two minutes.

(佳) The changes in the liquid pressure in the cylinder were measured every two minutes.

Unit 3　Academic Paper Writing

14. Classical, traditional, conventional

这些形容词的用法在某些情况下大同小异，但三个词的意思有些差异。Classical 这个词强调所指的理论或方法是经过时间的考验而证明为有价值的，被学者广为承认的。Traditional 是指"传统"或"惯例"，通常表示某个理论或方法使用已久，目前仍有人在使用，不过或许有人已经提出更新的理论或方法。Conventional 则表示时下最流行的理论与方法，而不反映这个理论与方法已存在多长时间。如：

(原句) The proposed architecture is more efficient than the traditional design, which was originally developed by researchers at IBM in 1993.

(修正句) The proposed architecture is more efficient than the conventional design, which was originally developed by researchers at IBM in 1993.

15. Due to

在标准的英文中，due to 只能用于修饰名词，以指出事情的原因。不要把 due to 当作介词引出原因状语并放在句首，这样的用法可以使用"owing to"或"because of"。如：

The accident was due to careless driving.

Owing to his careless driving, we had a bad accident.

Because of his careless driving, we had a bad accident.

16. equal

equal 为动词时，其后不能紧跟介词。Equal 为形容词时，其后必须加上介词 to。如：

(误) A kilometer equals to 1 000 meters.

(正) A kilometer is equal to 1 000 meters.

17. Famous

在科技论文中，使用 well-known 通常比使用 famous 恰当。如：

(不自然) A famous approach to constructing and maintaining information systems is introduced in the book by Steven Alter.

(自然) A well-known approach to constructing and maintaining information systems is introduced in the book by Steven Alter.

18. Give

give 是个意思不精确的词，要防止在科技论文中滥用 give。在大多数情况下，要表达"提出"，"给出"之意，使用 state, present 或 propose 这些意思较为精确的词要比使用 give 好得多。如：

(模糊) The concept of "Sequential Combustion" developed by ABB is given in this paper.

(精确) The concept of "Sequential Combustion" developed by ABB is presented/described/stated in this paper.

(模糊) First we will give the governing equations in the Cartesian coordinates.

(精确) First we will state/write the governing equations in the Cartesian coordinates.

19. Make

Make 是弱动词，它有很多用途。然而，除了一些固定的动宾搭配或短语外，为避免它的词义模糊，在科技论文中应尽量使用较特定的、具体的动词取代 make。如：

(模糊) Form the results of the experiment, the following conclusions can be made.

(精确) Form the results of the experiment, the following conclusions can be drawn.

(精确) The experimental results support the following conclusions.

20. Prove

除非指的是数学的证明，否则使用 prove 似乎显得过于强烈，应改用 confirm, verify 或其他词。如：

(差) Recent achievements in near room temperature magnetic refrigeration prove the effectiveness of the AMR cycle.

(佳) Recent achievements in near room temperature magnetic refrigeration confirm the effectiveness of the AMR cycle.

Unit 4

International Conference

Learning Objectives

In this unit, you will learn to accomplish the following tasks:

➤ Task 1: To know how to chair a meeting
➤ Task 2: To learn how to make a presentation
➤ Task 3: To familiarize asking and answering questions

Task 1: Chairing a Meeting

Format of Chairing a Meeting

- Opening the meeting
- Introducing the theme of the session
- Introducing oneself and co-chairperson
- Introducing the keynote speaker
- Complimenting on the speech
- Introducing the next speaker
- Closing the meeting

General Knowledge

1. Different sessions of the conference

There are different kinds of meetings held worldwide every year, including conference, symposium, seminar, forum, workshop, etc. An international conference, however, usually involves some different sessions, including an opening session, a plenary session, a presentation session, a discussion session, a closing session, etc. Therefore, there is usually more than one chairperson at an international conference, and different chairpersons responsible for different sessions may have different chairing duties.

Chairing different forms of meetings has different tasks. A plenary session is one at which all attendees of the conference are present. At a plenary session, there are always keynote speakers who deliver keynote speeches introducing the theme of the conference. Usually, only famous scholars or commonly recognized authorities in the field can be invited as keynote speakers. A presentation session is characterized by presentations delivered by different presenters. It is not always necessary for all the attendees of the conference to be present at a presentation session. Usually, only one group of attendees is present at a presentation session.

Unit 4 International Conference

The appropriate handling of a meeting depends on a chairman's adequate preparations, expertise in the topic of the meeting, past experiences, responsibilities and tactful chairing manners. This task only deals with how to chair a plenary session.

2. Chairmen's general duties

Usually, chairpersons are well-known scholars or authorities. A chairperson is supposed to be a good coordinator and organizer and able to cope with the changing situation properly. Since an international conference involves different sessions, we may have several chairpersons chairing these different sessions. We may have chairpersons of the opening and closing ceremony, chairpersons of a plenary session, chairpersons of a panel session and so on. All the chairpersons of these different sessions share some similar duties but slight variations do exist.

(1) A chairperson chairing the opening ceremony should:

Announce the opening of the conference;

Make a self-introduction;

Deliver welcoming words;

State the background, features, contents, and purposes of the conference;

Express good wishes to the conference as well as its attendees;

Introduce the speaker who is arranged to deliver a speech at the opening ceremony;

Thank the speaker, notice the next session time, and close the opening ceremony.

(2) A chairperson chairing a plenary session should:

Announce the beginning of the session;

Make a self-introduction;

Express the theme of the session;

Inform of the time limits and arrangements of the session;

Introduce a keynote speaker;

Control the question and answer session;

Thank the speaker and comment on the speaker's speech;

Introduce other keynote speakers and follow what has been done to the first speaker;

Notice the next session time and close the session.

(3) A chairperson chairing a presentation session should:

Announce the beginning of the session;

Make a self-introduction;

Express the topic of the session;

Inform of the rules and the time limits;

Introduce the first presenter;

Ask for questions and thank the presenter;

Introduce the last presenter, ask for questions, and thank the presenter;

Summarize and comment on the presentations;

Notice the next session time and close the session.

(4) A chairperson chairing a discussion session should:

Announce the beginning of the session;

Make a self-introduction;

Express the topic of the session;

Introduce the panelists and the rules;

Choose the questioners;

Choose the panelist to answer a question;

Control the time and the discussion;

Summarize the discussion, notice the next session time and close the session.

(5) A chairperson chairing the closing ceremony should:

Summarize the conference briefly;

Express thanks to all the related organizations and individuals;

Announce the next conference;

Announce the conference closed.

From the above introduction, we can see that a chairperson's general duties are: to invite the speakers, to moderate disagreements, if any, to keep the session in order, to control allocated time, and to create a pleasant atmosphere.

3. Opening a conference

A chairperson usually opens a conference by delivering an opening speech. We have discussed a little about opening speech early in this unit. An opening speech can be delivered either by the chairperson of the opening ceremony or sometimes by another well-known authority in the field. An opening speech generally consists of welcoming words to all the attendees, the thanks given to the related organizations and individuals, information about the background, features, contents, and purposes of the conference, and good wishes to the conference and its attendees.

4. Introducing a speaker

From the introduction of Part 1, we know that one of the general duties of a chairperson is to invite a speaker. Usually, when introducing a speaker, the chairperson mentions the speaker's academic experiences, achievements, position, research interest, etc. By mentioning such information, the chairperson aims to arouse the audience's curiosity about the speaker and to motivate the audience to like and show their respect for the speaker. Meanwhile, such an introduction may also make the audience respond favorably to the subsequent speech given by the speaker. At the end of the introduction, the chairperson announces the title of the speaker's presentation and delivers welcoming words to the speaker. There is one rule that the chairperson should bear in mind: The better known and more respected a speaker is, the shorter the chairperson's introduction should be; and the less well known a speaker is, the more the chairperson should arouse interest in the speaker's topic and make the audience show respect for the speaker.

Sample Demonstration

Sample 1

Distinguished Delegates and Guests, Ladies and Gentlemen, Good morning. I am Wu Wen from Beijing University. It is a great pleasure for me to share the chairmanship with Professor D. Harris from Stockholm, Sweden. On behalf of the organizing committee of HIV Treatment and Care in the New Century, I would like to announce the session open.

We have some of the world's foremost clinicians, basic scientists, and researchers at the forefront of this field. Let me introduce our first speaker—Professor Michael Saag, who is a Director of the University of Alabama AIDS Outpatient Clinic in Birmingham, Alabama.

He's also the Associate Director of Clinical Care and Therapeutics at the University of Alabama AIDS Center. Professor Saag has published extensively in medical journals and books on the subject of the basic science of HIV and clinical treatment of HIV. He's extensively involved in AIDS treatment and policy, and his presentation is entitled "Current Controversies in Antiviral Therapy".

...

Thank you, Prof. Saag. Your presentation is very convincing. From your presentation, we know that you back up the Dutch theory, that is, antiviral drugs are not preventing HIV from killing cells, but simply releasing into the blood mature CD4 cells that have been trapped elsewhere. If the Dutch team is right, the consequences could be profound, and scientists will find new ways of treatment for people with HIV infection in the new century. Your speech is indeed very useful, interesting and challengeable. Thank you.

OK, let me introduce the next speaker Prof. Alan Simpson.

...

Sample 2

Ladies and Gentlemen:

Good evening. As the chairperson of this Millionaire Mind Seminar, I have the pleasure and honor of welcoming all of you. We have an excellent session for you, in terms of both content and the distinction and the stature of our speakers. The first speaker is Richard Allan Carswell, who is one of the most popular professional speakers in the world today! Each year he addresses tens of thousands of men and women on the subjects of leadership, negotiation, selling, and personal and business success.

As a best-selling author, and an extraordinary trainer on personal and professional development, Mr. Richard Carswell believes that each person has an enormous untapped reservoir of potential that he or she can access to achieve more, be more, and ultimately have more in just a few years than the average person does in an entire lifetime. Today Mr. Carswell's presentation title is "From Success to Significance". If you want to discover your innate, inner capacity to create permanent wealth, and more significantly, to keep your wealth and grow it

Unit 4 International Conference

exponentially, please join me in welcoming this outstanding speaker—Mr. Richard Carswell!

…

Thank you, Mr.Carswell. Your speech is absolutely pure gold, and very inspiring. We are delighted to be able to share your new specific strategies and techniques. I think everyone wants to be a millionaire, to make a big fortune. The secrets of creating fortune and success will greatly cherish the people present here.

I'd like to pay my tribute to the speakers for their excellent presentations and the audience for their attention this evening. I declare the plenary session adjourned until 10 a.m.

Useful Expressions and Sentence Patterns

1. To open the introduction（开场白）

(1) It is my great pleasure to introduce our speaker today, Dr. Smith.

(2) We are fortunate today to have Dr. Liu with us.

(3) I am delighted to make a few introductory remarks about our first speaker today, Prof. Jones.

(4) It's my privilege to introduce our keynote speaker, HojjatAdeli, to you.

(5) I am delighted to make a few introductory remarks about our keynote speaker.

2. To introduce the speaker's position（介绍发言人现任职务）

(1) The first special lecture will be presented by Dr. John D. Anthony, Professor of Telecommunication at Boston University.

(2) Our next speaker is Dr. Wood. He has been working at the University of Oxford.

(3) Dr. Kenner is currently the president of the American Food and Drug Association.

(4) Our keynote speaker is the president of the American Committee on Jerusalem, as well as the past president of the Middle East Studies Association and an advisor to the Palestinian delegation to the Madrid and Washington Arab-Israeli peace negotiations from October 1991 to June 1993. He is also, as many of you

know, a professor of Middle East history and director of the Center for International Studies at the University of Chicago.

3. To introduce the speaker's education background（介绍发言人学历）

(1) Our speaker got her Ph. D. from Georgia State University, master's from Boston College, and a nursing degree from Oxford University.

(2) Six years of post-graduate study in natural health has led him to convey a unique understanding of health and nutrition. Graduating with honors, he has formal training and experience to empower others with a straightforward message of health and wellness.

(3) Nancy earned her Master's Degree from Bowing Green State University in Ohio and graduated Magna Cum Laude from Oswego State University in New York.

(4) Terry holds a Bachelor of Science degree in communications. He also holds a Master of Business Administration in marketing from Georgia State University.

4. To introduce the speaker's academic/educational and professional experiences（介绍发言人学术、工作经历）

(1) With a Ph. D. (1995) in computational intelligence applied to systems diagnostics under the illustrious supervision of Professor Rolf Isermann at Darmstadt University of Technology, Germany, Dr. Ulieru started her academic career as Lecturer in Computer Science and Information Systems at Brunel University, London, UK. A postdoctoral fellowship (1997) with Prof. William Gruver in the Intelligent Manufacturing and Robotics Group at Simon Fraser University brought her to Canada where she was awarded the Junior Nortel Chair at the University of Calgary in 1998.

(2) Dr. Oleg Gusikhin received his Ph. D. from St. Petersburg Institute of Informatics and Automation of the Russian Academy of Sciences in 1992. Since 1993, he has been working at Ford Motor Company in different functional areas of the company including Information Technology, Advanced Electronics Manufacturing, and Research &- Advanced Engineering.

(3) Norihiro Hagita received B.S., M.S. and Ph. D. degrees in electrical engineering from Keio University (Japan) in 1976, 1978 and 1986 respectively. He

joined NTT during 1978-1988. In 1996 through 2001, he served as an executive manager in NTT Communication Science Labs. Soon after he moved to ATR, he established new laboratories which are called the ATR Media Information Science Labs in October, 2001, and the ATR Intelligent Robotics and Communication laboratories on Oct. 2002.

5. To introduce the speaker's academic achievements and publications（介绍发言人学术成果，发表文章或著作）

(1) Dr. John D. Anthony is an editor or author of numerous chapters in many of our textbooks. His AI book, Artificial Intelligence: Structures and Strategies for Complex Problem Solving (Addison-Wesley 2005) is now into its fifth edition.

(2) Professor Mark is best known for developing the SMART Agent Framework with Michael Luck using techniques from formal methods. Much of this research can be found in a book entitled Understanding Agent Systems, which is now in its second edition and published earlier this year with Springer. He also co-authored a further book published in 2004 called Agent-based Software Development. He has collaborated with many leading agent researchers and has published over 70 papers in this area.

(3) Hojjat Adeli has authored over 400 researches and scientific publications in various fields of computer science, engineering, and applied mathematics since 1976 when he received his Ph. D. from Stanford University at the age of 26. He has authored ten books including Machine Learning—Neural Networks, Genetic Algorithms, and Fuzzy Systems, Wiley, 1995 ... He has also edited twelve books including Knowledge Engineering, Fundamentals, Applications, McGraw-Hill, 1990.

6. To introduce the speaker's research focus（介绍发言人的科研方向及领域）

(1) Gene Myers's research interests include the design of algorithms, pattern matching, computer graphics, and computational molecular biology. His most recent academic work has focused on algorithms for the central combinatorial problems involved in DNA sequencing and on a wide range of sequence and pattern comparison problems.

(2) Mihaela Ulieru's current research is focused on distributed intelligent environments (coined as "ambient intelligence") and their applications to e-Health, emergency response management and intelligent manufacturing.

(3) The research interests of Professor Robert Engle are financial econometrics, time series analysis, volatility and risk management, and empirical market microstructure.

7. To introduce the awards gained by the speaker（介绍发言人所获奖项）

(1) In 1998 HojjatAdeli received the Distinguished Scholar Award from the OhioStateUniversity in recognition of extraordinary accomplishment in research and scholarship.

(2) Mihaela Ulieru's extensive work with the industry earned her the Chairmanship of the 1st IEEE International Conference on Industrial Informatics in 2003.

(3) Gene Myers was awarded the IEEE 3rd MilleniumAcheivernent Award in 2000, the Nezvcomb Cleveland Best Paper in Science award in 2001, and the ACM Kanellakis Prize in 2002. He was voted the most influential in bioinformatics in 2001 by Genome Technology Magazine and was elected to the National Academy of Engineering in 2003. In 2004 he won the International Max-Planck Research Prize.

8. To introduce the topic of the speaker's presentation（介绍发言人发言话题）

(1) The title of Professor Luger's talk today is "Diagnosis and Prognosis: From Rule-Based Systems to First-Order Graphical Models".

(2) Today Professor Robert Engle is going to talk on "Dynamic Conditional correlation—A Simple Class Of Multivariate GARCH Models".

(3) I am happy to present to you our speaker, Professor Robert Engle, who will now address you on "The Econometrics of Ultra High Frequency Data".

(4) So to speak to you on "Autoregressive Conditional Duration", please welcome Dr. Lee.

9. To welcome the speaker（向发言人表示欢迎）

(1) Now ladies and gentlemen, please join me in welcoming Professor Robert Engle.

(2) Ladies and gentlemen, would you please join me in welcoming our guest speaker today, Professor Luger?

(3) If you would, please help me give a warm welcome to our keynote speaker, Mihaela Ulieru.

(4) Now, I would like to extend a warm welcome to our first speaker, Hojjat Adeli.

Task 2: Making a Presentation

Format of Making a Presentation

◆ Preparing the presentation
◆ Beginning the presentation
◆ Developing the presentation
◆ Ending the presentation

General Knowledge

In the previous unit, we have been informed of enough knowledge about how to write an academic paper; however, in this unit, we should first know how different a speech is from an article. In order to make a good presentation at a conference, a speaker needs to do some preparatory work for it and to rehearse beforehand. When starting to present, the speaker should have some knowledge about how to open and end a presentation. During the presentation, the speaker should know how to introduce a topic, how to move to another topic, how to describe the involved research, how to skip or omit some parts, how to correct oral or written mistakes, and how to summarize the topic.

1. Preparing the presentation

Since a speaker is given limited time to present his or her speech at a conference, he or she has to make good preparations for it. Here we will talk about three major things that a speaker needs to prepare for a presentation.

(1) Bad conference presentations.

You must have seen poor conference presentations. The speaker walks to the front and sits down at the table. You cannot see him because people are in front of you. He starts reading from his paper in a dead, low voice, which is difficult to hear. His sentences are long, complex and filled with technical words and phrases. He emphasizes complicated details, so you lose his point. With five minutes left in the session, the speaker suddenly looks at his watch. He announces that he will have to leave out the most important points because time is running out. He becomes confused. He continues to talk. Fifteen minutes after the scheduled end of the talk, the host reminds the speaker for the third time to finish. Finally, the speaker cannot think of anything else to say and asks for questions.

(2) Principles of effective conference presentations.

Listening to presentations is hard work. Especially at conferences, where audiences listen for hours, people need the speaker to help them focus. An effective talk must do three things: Persuade your audience with evidence, be interesting, and be entertaining.

Conference presenters usually use persuasive evidence, but forget to be interesting. Some speakers think the evidence, by itself, is interesting. It is not. Some speakers believe that being interesting is not an appropriate conference goal. Some speakers believe that if a talk is interesting and easy to follow, it is not important. These speakers are mistaken. It is impossible to persuade without being interesting. Keeping people interested and involved is important because to communicate your research, being interesting is not about making your audience laugh, and taking away their troubles, but simply about keeping them focused on, and interested in what you have to say.

- Talk, instead of reading

Written academic language is more complex than conversation. Sentences are long, with many clauses and technical vocabulary that are impossible to follow when reading aloud. Academic writing does not make good speaking. If you just talk, it will be easier to understand, and you will connect with your audience. You will think more clearly. If you cannot communicate your points without reading, do you really know your points? Many beginning presenters forget that listening to someone read from a slide is worse than listening to them read a paper. Your audience will read the entire slide in the first 30 seconds, much faster than you can read it aloud. Do not bore them by reading. Instead, use the slide to remind you of what to say. Speak about the slide instead of reading it. If you must read, keep your reading text separate from your slides.

- Stand up

If people are sitting in rows, stand up, even if there are only a few. This lets people in the back rows see your face and hear you better. If you cannot see their faces, they cannot see yours. Remember, you are the focus. The audience wants to see you.

- Move around

It is easier to keep the focus on someone who is moving than on a motionless talking head. Hand gestures are good, too. Show your enthusiasm for your topic. Simply walking from one side of the room to the other every three to four minutes is usually enough.

- Make eye contact with your audience

If this makes you afraid, pretend to make eye contact by looking around the room. People will think you are looking at someone, even if you only look at the wall just above their heads. Or, find a few friendly faces at different places in the room and speak directly to them, changing from one face to another.

Speakers usually concentrate on those who are nodding or smiling. This is a good way to maintain confidence. However, remember that it is often the people who are frowning, falling asleep, or bored whom you need to include. If looking at them makes you nervous, use the technique of looking around the room over the audience's heads.

- Do not look at one side of the room only

Many speakers do this without thinking about it, always looking to the left or the right half, or only to the front or the back of the room. A projector forces you to stand far to one side or the other. Avoid this by moving from one side of the screen to the other.

- Imitate excellent speakers

The best way to become an excellent speaker is to watch experienced speakers and copy their presentation style. Academia is full of bad speakers, so you may have to look hard to find a great role model. When you do find role models, notice not just what they say, but what they do: How they move, how they use their voices, and how to look at the audience, how they handle timing and questions. It is important to find someone in your field to imitate. Political speaking styles or television styles do not work well in an academic environment. If you find an excellent model and work hard to copy that person, you cannot go wrong. Your own style will come in time.

(3) A short conference talk outline.

This conference talk outline is a basic template. Most speakers average two minutes per slide, not including the title and outline slides, and use about 12 slides for a 20-minute presentation.

Title/Author/University (1 slide)

Abstract (1 slide)

Give the basic problem and answer. What is the one idea you want people to leave?

Outline (1 slide)

Give the talk structure. Some speakers prefer to put his at the bottom of their title slide.

Motivation and problem statements (1-2 slides)

Why does anyone care? Most researchers overestimate how much the audience knows about their problem.

Related work (0-1 slide)

Talk briefly about this, or you can eliminate this section and refer people to your paper.

Methods (1 slide)

Cover quickly in short talks and refer people to your paper.

Results (4-6 slides)

Present key results with implications. This is the main body of the talk. The structure depends on the researcher's contribution. Do not cover all the results. Cover the key result well. Do not just present numbers, but instead interpret them to give applications. Do not put up large tables of numbers.

Summary

Future Work (0-1 slide)

Or, you can talk about additional problems coming from this research.

Backup Slides (0-3 slides)

You may have a few slides ready to answer expected questions. Possible question areas are ideas you quickly go over, limitations in the methods or results, and future work.

2. Rehearsing the presentation

Before coming to the conference to make a presentation, a speaker should rehearse it beforehand. By rehearsing the presentation in the front of those who may give suggestions to him or her, a speaker can find out whether his or her tone, pronunciation of each word, including some symbols such as "+", "/", etc., pace of delivery, posture, etc. are appropriate or not and make some adjustments in time. In addition, through more and more rehearsing, the speaker will become more and more familiar with the presentation script and can gain more and more confidence.

3. Delivering the speech

After preparing and rehearsing the presentation, a speaker should confidently come to the conference, overcome his or her nervousness, and present the speech.

During the Presentation, the Speaker Should Know

- How to greet and address the audience;
- How to thank the chairperson and the hosts for giving him or her the opportunity to present the paper;
- How to make a self-introduction;
- How to introduce the topic and begin the presentation;
- How to develop the presentation;
- How to skip or omit some parts to make full use of the limited time;
- How to correct some oral or written mistakes that may occur;
- How to summarize and end the presentation.

Steps

Step 1: Beginning the presentation

In the following parts of this section, we will go into detail about the above-mentioned aspects of delivering each part of a speech. A good beginning of a presentation should first be able to catch the audience's attention and arouse their interest. Make sure you get it right and start your speech strong.

- Step 1 Be familiar with your material and any facts, names, or numbers you are planning to use. If you are looking down or moving papers, you will lose your audience and any energy or confidence you had. Practice until you are completely comfortable with your subject.

- Step 2 Walk to the stage and smile. Be quiet for at least three seconds while looking at your audience and smile. This will immediately connect your audience as they are waiting to see what will happen next, and it shows you as a confident speaker with a good speech.

- Step 3 Start with a quote, a story, a number, or a fact, preferably something that is surprising or unusual, that your audience has not heard before. Opening with a statement and launching into your speech is much more interesting than "Welcome ladies and gentlemen" or "I am going to talk about", which your audience has heard many times before.

- Step 4 Think of the speech opening like the beginning of a good movie. Use the first two minutes to build excitement. The best way to do this is to use surprising facts or a story. This will build the base and involve people creating interest in seeing where you will take them.

- Step 5 Keep related thoughts together and avoid moving to different topics or areas of your speech. Keep your thoughts and subject organized. It will make it much easier for people to follow what you are saying. It will make the beginning of your speech more enjoyable.

Eight Techniques to Start with and Get Attention

1. Ask a question

"Is it safe to trust documents from the Internet?"
"Is there anyone here who has not broken the copyright law?"

2. Use a story

Many of the best stories are personal.

3. Make a surprising comment (often a statistic)

"According to a national survey reported in the Wall Street Journal, 82% of respondents say they access pornography on the Net at work."

4. Use a quotation

"Confucius said: 'What I hear I forget, what I see I remember, what I do I understand.' We need to use this method, as I planned an interactive class."

Choose a quote from movies, speeches, newspapers, reports, official documents, or use a quotation book.

5. Create curiosity

"There is a position in your home. Your children use it and so do you. It kills thousands every year. Yet the government does not control it. Here it is table salt."

6. Mention the importance of the topic

"With 400,000 job openings for computer professionals in the United States, it is important that we train computer professionals now. I have a plan that will do this quickly and with little expense."

7. Involve the audience

Ask for participation in a survey. Or, show a picture or short video and ask for the audience's comments.

8. Refer to the occasion

Speech is often part of a special event for a group, organization, or community. Connect any special celebrations to your topic.

A good Beginning of a Presentation Should Indicate

(1) Opening remarks (including: thanks to the chairperson, greetings to the audiences, expression of the pleasure).

(2) Icebreaker: anecdote, story, questions to catch the audience's attention.

(3) Introduction of the topic, the purpose, the background information, the outline of the speech, the time needed, etc.

(4) Turning to the first point of the presentation.

The beginning of a speech is the most important. It either connects with your audience from the start or gives them a reason to ignore you.

Sample Demonstration

Step 1: Beginning the presentation

Sample 1

Honorable Under-Secretary-General,
Mr. Ocampo, Ambassador Nirupam Sen, and Distinguished Guests,

It is a privilege and an honor to be invited at the United Nations to deliver a talk on "Global Imbalances: an Indian Perspective". I would like to thank Professor Jose Antonio Ocampo, Under-Secretary-General, for inviting me to deliver this talk. In my presentation today, I hope to capture the debate among the policymakers as well as academics; though I must be humble in the presence of Mr. Ocampo who has been a Minister, and a Professor and currently international civil servant of eminence. To benefit from the discussions that are expected to follow, I will restrict my presentation to about 15 to 20 minutes.

First, I would like to reflect upon the international perspective on global imbalances by raising three issues: (a) the essential features of the global imbalances as they stand today, (b) possible causes of these imbalances, and (c) the emerging consensus on policy responses.

Second, I will attempt to highlight India's perspective on the global imbalances. While doing l so' I would try to cover the following aspects: (a) India's role in global imbalances, (b) approach to global consensus on causes and policy responses, (c) possible impact of global imbalances on India, and (d) the emergence of oil as a new factor in the policy debate on global imbalances.

Third, I shall explore a possible agenda for analysis to enable a better understanding of global imbalances.

(Now, let's come to "Global Perspective on Global Imbalances" ...)

Step 2: Developing the Presentation

The body of the speech is between the beginning and the end. Although each speech part has a unique function and is important, the body is the biggest and requires some imagination to organize effectively. Organizers connect concepts or themes, such as characters, place, size, or time.

The time to consider the way to organize the body of your speech is after you brainstorm and choose your points. Organizers make it easier for the audience to understand and remember what you say. Organizers make it easier to connect your opening, body structure, and ending as a unit. They provide the structure to connect your ideas, help you connect with the audience quickly, and deliver the speech with minimal notes.

You have many organizational options and the previously mentioned "three points" or "three reasons" is only one. When considering different ways to organize the body of the speech, remember that the speech body has three to five parts, at most. Even stories should be told in parts. Audiences can take in a limited amount of information at one time.

Unlike the written word, which is designed for future reference, speeches are temporary and need to use a human's natural ability to make connections. Give the audience an overview of your organization, along with your goals, in your introduction.

When developing the presentation, you may:

(1) Present your main points one by one in a logical order.

(2) Pause at the end of each point (give people time to take notes or time to think about what you are saying).

(3) Make it absolutely clear when you move to another point. For example: "The next point is that ...".

(4) Use clear examples to illustrate your points.

Sample 2

(Introductory Part ...)

Now, let's come to "Global Perspective on Global Imbalances" in the first place.

The first subpoint of this part is Essential Feature of the Global Imbalances.

It is useful to understand that in different countries the existence of a current account surplus or deficit is inevitable among economies at any given time. In particular, one of the arguments in favor of global integration is that capital may flow from developed economies to the capital-starved developing economies which imply that there would be current account deficits in the latter. The problem is not the existence of current account deficits or surpluses per se, but it is the persistence of large current account deficit and large current account surplus, particularly in large and systemically important economies, which give rise to fears of unsustainability and disruptive unwinding.

The second subpoint I'd like to talk about is Possible Causes of Global Imbalances.

The current global imbalance is reflected in large mismatches in the current account positions in some countries and its mirror image in the form of domestic saving-investment mismatches. ... Under such a scenario (模式), it has been felt, many of these countries tried to maintain their external price competitiveness by keeping their currencies undervalued. The process, it is stated, in turn, led to large trade and current account surplus for the Asian EMEs and large trade and current deficits elsewhere in the world, most noticeably in the US.

The last subpoint in this part is The Emerging Consensus on Policy Responses.

As regards the current global initiatives to correct global imbalances, the Communiqué (公报) issued by the International Monetary and Financial Committee (IMFC) released on April 22, 2006 highlights that action for orderly medium-term resolution of global imbalances is a shared responsibility, and will bring greater benefit to members and the international community than actions taken individually by countries. Key elements of the strategy towards orderly resolution of the global imbalance suggested in the Communiqué are as follows:

raising national saving in the United States-with measures to

(1) reduce the budget deficit and spur private saving;

(2) ...

(3) ...

(4) ...

(5) promoting efficient absorption of higher oil strong macroeconomic policies.

Now let's move on to the next main point "India's Perspective on Global Imbalances".

First, I'd like to talk about India's Role in Global Imbalances. Since Independence, India has moved from a moderate growth path of the first three decades (1950 to 1980) to a higher growth trajectory（轨道）since the 1980s …

In this context, it is appropriate to view the evidence that the policies followed by India have not in any way contributed to the widening of the current global imbalances:

First, between 2001-2002 and 2003-2004, India registered modest current account surpluses, but this was more of a reflection phase of the business cycle, and with the turnaround in the Laziness cycle, India has registered a modest current account deficit in the last two years. In fact, going by the current indication and the projections of the tenth Five Year Plan, India is likely to maintain a modest and sustainable current account deficit in the near future.

Second, our approach aimed at market-determined exchange rate with no predetermined target along with market interventions essentially to manage volatility has served us well. … Recent international research on viable exchange rate emerging markets has lent considerable support to the exchange rate policy followed by India.

Third, the overall improvement in GDP growth during the reform period has also been facilitated by improvement in the rate of aggregate domestic saving. For instance, in the high growth phase of the last three years, the saving rate rose by 5.5 percentage points from 23.5 percent in 2001-2002 to 29. 1 percent in 2004-2005…

India has, thus, been following policies which not only served it well but also contributed to global stability. As mentioned by our Finance Minister, Mr. P. Chidambaram, we do not expect any change in the basic framework of our policies both in terms of growth based on efficient use of capital and stability assured by sound macroeconomic policies.

The second point in this part is The Approach to Global Consensus on Causes and Policy Responses. We view that global developments, particularly those in the world financial markets, have the most direct and serious impact on the financing conditions in the emerging markets. Any abrupt and disorderly adjustment to global imbalances may have serious adverse implications.

At this juncture, it is appropriate to list some important considerations that should govern. Initiatives in regard to the resolution of global imbalances recognizing that such policy initiatives may be broadly in consonance（一致）with emerging consensus described earlier in the address.

First, it is necessary for multilateral institutions like IMF to be seen as symmetrical（对称的）in their analysis of national economies and their relative positions in the global economy. This would add credibility to the policy advice that could be considered by each country.

Second, at the same time, action by each country will be governed by enlightened national interest. It is necessary for multilateral institutions to analyze, explore and convince how the policy actions would serve the long-term national interest.

Third, it is desirable to convince the policymakers in each country that actions considered appropriate are in the long-term interest of the country itself. In this regard, the contextual challenges for each economy should be given due weight. For example, in countries like India, employment and poverty reduction need to be given the highest priority.

The third subpoint, I'd like to analyze Possible Impact of Global Imbalances on India. India does not depend on the international capital market for financing the fiscal deficit and]consequently to some extent adverse consequences of the global developments would be muted（减弱）. However, there could be a spill-over（伴随的结果）effect of global developments on domestic interest rates and thus on fisc also. The fiscal position of the Government could also be indirectly impacted through the nature of management of foreign exchange reserves held by the Reserve Bank.

Similarly, any abrupt adjustment in global imbalances may affect corporates, banks, and households in India, though the impact may be less than some other emerging economies.

The last subpoint in this part concerns The Emergence of Oil as a New Factor. The emergence of large current account surpluses among the oil exporting countries is an important recent development…

In this regard, it may be noted that India's oil import bill amounted to 2.9 percent of GDP in 2001-2002, but the bill climbed to 5.5 percent of GDP in 2005-2006, though in volume terms the increase has been marginal.

Ladies and gentlemen, the last main point is an "Agenda for Analysis".

In view of the complex nature of global imbalances and the way forward to minimize the risks of disorderly adjustments, it may be useful to explore possible agenda for further analysis.

First, national balance sheets, as mentioned by Governor Mervyn King, could be given special attention to get a fuller picture of financial claims that countries have against other countries. Looking at the national balance sheets would also be useful to acquire a sense about the potential for adjustment, and they will give a sense of the possible impact of relative price changes on the value of assets and liabilities…

Second, following the experience of the East Asian crisis of 1997-1998, vulnerabilities rather than public sector imbalances played a key role in precipitating(促成)the crisis, the third generation models have explicitly brought to the fore the role of balance sheet mismatches in causing financial crises… It would, therefore, be useful to analyze the impact of global imbalances on various balance sheets within the country such as the government sector, financial sector including banks and financial institutions, non-financial private sector including corporates and households.

Third, as mentioned earlier, the surplus of oil exporting countries has emerged as a new factor in the debate on the global imbalance… Such inflows could have helped to keep long-term interest rates as also emerging market bond spreads low, even as policy rates are rising. An interesting issue would be the nature of their responses to the unwinding of global imbalances.

Finally, is it possible that there are several intermediate scenarios between and disruptive or disorderly adjustments? A series of marginal adjustments, often in spurts（迸发），could take place which may appear random but move towards the gradual lessening of imbalances through an interactive and iterative（反复的）processes encompassing markets, national policies, and global cooperation. The agenda for analysis proposed here may facilitate exploration of such intermediate scenarios of unwinding global imbalances.

(Conclusion...)

Step 3: Ending the presentation

An energetic ending is critical to a successful presentation because the last thing said is what the audience remembers best. It is where you emphasize your main message. Your presentation will die early with a bad conclusion like, "Well, I see I have run out of time" or "I don't have anything more to say." You can avoid dead endings by following a simple preparation and delivery template. It works for all types of presentations including teaching.

A good end of a presentation should:

(1) Signals that the presentation comes to the end.

(2) Summarize the presentation briefly.

(3) End it directly by thanking the chairperson.

Sample 3

To conclude, the performance of the Indian economy since 1980, and in particular since the reforms in the 1990s, is in many ways an impressive success story both in terms of growth and stability. The Indian economy has responded well to the rising global competition with gradually increasing integration with the world economy. The current high growth phase of the Indian economy is also coinciding with rising domestic saving rates. While India by itself hardly contributes to the current global financial imbalances, any large and rapid adjustments in major currencies and related interest rates or current accounts of trading partners could indirectly, but significantly, impact the Indian economy. We, therefore, have a large stake in the process of the unwinding of global imbalances, and we are willing to play our part in ensuring successful outcomes from current initiatives.

Thank you.

Useful Expressions and Sentence Patterns

1. To greet and address the audience

(1) Excellencies, distinguished participants, ladies, and gentlemen.

(2) Fellow delegates, ladies and gentlemen.

(3) Distinguished guests, friends, ladies, and gentlemen.

(4) Respected Honorary President Dr. Wood, distinguished colleagues.

2. To catch attention and arouse interest

(1) Good morning, ladies and gentlemen. I'd like to start my presentation with a question. Do you know how much actual meat there is in a hot dog? (Asking a question)

(2) Ladies and gentlemen, good morning! I am here to talk to you about a disease, some of you may already be affected; most of you will in some way be touched by this disease. If this disease can't be eradicated, it will have a direct and serious impact on every person in this room! (Making a startling statement)

(3) Good afternoon, everyone! There is a Chinese saying "with a hare under one's garment" to describe the uneasiness for a nervous person. That is how I am feeling at such a moment, and before such a big audience, there seems to be a hare under my garment. Well, now speaking about "nervous", I would like to show you the results of my experiment on the nervous system of rabbit … (Using a quotation)

(4) Mr. Chairman, distinguished delegates, ladies, and gentlemen, good morning! Today I'd like to talk about the MIS in China. But don't be mistaken – the "MIS in China，is not a young lady in China. MIS is a short form for Management Information System. It is an integrated user-machine system for providing information to support operations management, and decision-making functions in an organization ... (Telling something humorous)

(5) I know you've all traveled a long way to come here to attend this conference. (Referring to the audience)

(6) An interesting thing happened on my way to this conference... (Relating an anecdote)

3. To express pleasure and honor（表达喜悦和荣幸）

(1) It is an honor and a pleasure for me to have this opportunity to meet with many friends of ASEAN and China who are the key players, true supporters and valuable partners in strengthening cooperation and promoting the continued growth and prosperity between the two regions.

(2) It is a privilege and an honor to be invited at the United Nations to deliver a talk on "Global Imbalances: an Indian Perspective".

(3) I am glad to avail myself of this opportunity to exchange and discuss with all of you on the prospects of the China-ASEAN Free Trade Area.

(4) I am very pleased to have this opportunity of presenting my study on system engineering.

(5) It is a great pleasure to speak about semiconductor research in China in this session of the conference.

4. To express thanks to the chairperson or the hosts（向会议主持人或主办方致谢）

(1) Please allow me to briefly express my deep appreciation to the people and government of China, particularly the Government of Yunnan province, for the excellent arrangements and cordial hospitality in hosting this important conference.

(2) I would like to thank Professor Jose Antonio Ocampo, Under-Secretary-General, for inviting me to deliver this talk.

(3) Mr. Chairman, thank you for your introduction.

(4) First of all, I'd like to start by thanking our hosts for inviting me to come to this beautiful country.

(5) Thank you very much, Prof. Lee, for your very kind introduction.

5. To indicate the topics, purposes, and outline of the presentation（表明演讲的话题、目的及主要内容和结构）

(1) What I am going to present today are the methodology and the data analysis.

(2) My topic today will deal with the effects of this medicine on patients.

(3) I shall devote my talk to the liberation of women in the 20th century.

(4) I want to confine my talk to the literature on that topic.

(5) In my presentation today, I hope to capture the debate among the policymakers as well as academics...

(6) My presentation will be given in four parts. The first part deals with... The second part relates to... The third part concerns... And the last part discusses...

6. To shift to another topic（话题转换）

(1) Well, let's move on to the next point.

(2) So much for the methodology of our experiment. I would now like to shift to the discussion of the results.

(3) That brings me to a second important issue.

(4) Now let's move away from the first part and switch over to the next part of my presentation.

(5) Turning to the next part, I'd like to talk about the causes of such a problem.

(6) Let's come back to what I have talked about in the first part of my speech.

(7) To come back to the first part of my speech, I suggest that…

(8) At this point, I'd like to refer again to what I said at the beginning of my presentation.

7. To elaborate on something（详细讨论某话题）

(1) I suppose this part is the most difficult, so let's discuss it at length.

(2) Since this is a key problem, I'd like to go into some detail.

(3) I'd like to deal with the third part of my presentation more extensively.

(4) I shall talk about this difficult problem in detail.

(5) As to the last point of my presentation, I'd like to spend more minutes on it.

8. To brief on something（略谈某话题）

(1) I'm not going to go into detail on this subject.

(2) I shall not discuss it in depth.

(3) I won't go over this subject in detail.

(4) I don't think I should spend much time describing this part.

(5) Since this point is quite easy for you to understand, I will talk about it briefly.

9. To amend a slip of tongue or correct some mistakes（修正口误、错误）

(1) The number is 14 million, sorry, 40 million.

(2) Now let's move to the second point, sorry, the third.

(3) The temperature increased, I shall say decreased.

(4) Now let me show you the lights, I mean the slides.

(5) As you can see from the first line on the slide, excuse me, the second line.

10. To signal the end of the presentation and summarize briefly the main ideas of the presentation（示意论文宣读即将结束并简要总结论文主要思想）

(1) To end, I would like to present the last slide to you.

(2) Now I'd like to summarize my talk.

(3) To close my speech, I would like to sum up the major points I have already made.

(4) Well, that brings me to the end of my presentation. This last slide is a brief summary of what I have talked about.

(5) In conclusion, I'd like to emphasize the following points.

11. To end the presentation in a common way（以普通方式结束论文宣读）

(1) That's the end of my presentation. Thank you for your attention.

(2) So much for my presentation. Thank you.

(3) That concludes my presentation. Thank you for listening.

(4) That's all. Thank you very much.

12. To end the presentation in other ways（以其他方式结束论文宣读）

(1) I would like to end the presentation by quoting a famous Chinese saying…

(2) Let me close by quoting Shakespeare, the great English playwright, and poet, who said that…

(3) I'd like to come to a close by quoting a poem from the great Chinese poet, Li Bai…

(4) We look forward to working closely with NGOs and other civil society organizations in reducing poverty and improving the living standards of the people…

(5) We believe, with joint efforts of different countries, renewable energy will surely develop faster and better and will play a promotional role in global sustainable development.

13. To express thanks to the chairperson or the hosts（向会议主持人或主办方致谢）

(1) Without taking any longer time of the conference, I would like to express my sincere appreciation once again to the host of this conference which provides me wonderful opportunities to exchange views and comments on ways to further strengthen trade and economic between ASEAN and China.

(2) Finally Mr. Chairman, I would like to take the opportunity to thank the Chinese government, especially, the Yunnan Provincial Government, for sponsoring and organizing this conference and the excellent arrangements they have made.

14. To invite questions and comments （邀请提问或评价）

(1) Thank you for your attention. I would be glad to address your questions now.

(2) That's all for my presentation. Please don't hesitate to ask me if you have any questions.

Tips for Making a Presentation

Because of your concerns or nervousness, you may unknowingly engage in behavior that may detract from your speech. Behavior that can detract from your presentation include:

(1) Avoiding eye contact with the audience.

Looking at the ceiling, out the window, at the floor, or at the camera

Staring at one member of the audience, or at only one section of the room

Looking at notes to avoid eye contact with the audience

If you think you may have trouble establishing eye contact with the audience or tend to focus on only one or two listeners, try dividing the audience into three or four groups. Move your eyes from one group to another, making sure to include the groups to your far left and far right. If you feel uncomfortable looking directly at people's eyes, look at another part of their face, such as their nose.

(2) Making distracting body movements.

Pulling on your shirtsleeve

Pacing back and forth or shuffling your feet

Taking your hands in and out of your pockets

Playing with objects in your hand (papers, transparencies, pens, keys, etc.)

(3) Avoiding the use of hand gestures.

Grasping your hands behind your back or in front of you

Keeping your hands in your pockets or "glued" to your side

Holding something in your hands, such as a pen, large piece of paper, or pointer

(4) Other distracting behaviors.

Laughing nervously

Gum chewing or snapping

Task 3: Asking and Answering Questions

Format of Asking and Answering Questions

- ◆ Declaring the session open
- ◆ Asking questions
- ◆ Answering questions
- ◆ Declaring the session closed

General Knowledge

In a Question and Answer session, a chairperson is supposed to call on the participants to raise questions, to remind the speakers of the topics on the agenda if the speakers go far away from them, to moderate disagreements between speakers and questioners that may occur during the discussion, to keep the session in order, to summarize the discussion, and to thank the speakers and the audience. Speakers need to answer questions clearly and actively. Asking and answering questions play a dominant role in academic speeches, specialized discussions, and dissertation defenses. Questions exert influence on the speakers in that they reveal whether the speakers can provide the requested information or not, what kind of information can be offered on the spot, and in what way it is given. Questions and answers get attention, create interest, generate feedback, make points easy to remember, create audience interaction, and promote new thoughts.

1. Types of questions in Q & A sessions

During the process of a discussion session (or an oral defense), the audience may raise various kinds of questions, which, according to their motivation, purposes, and requirements, could be classified into the following types.

(1) Questions for clarifying problems.

The discussion session provides the audience with an opportunity to clarify the points that they have not quite understood or that have not been fully demonstrated, to ask for some statistical information, etc. For example,

Mr.Chairman, I'd like to ask Mr...what he refers to by getting a peak value.

I don't quite understand what you really mean by saying... Can you explain it again?

I would like to ask you a question, or rather, make a request. Is it possible...?

Could you please tell me how many...?

(2) Questions for showing special interest.

The listeners also ask questions in order to learn more details about a particular aspect or to have a deeper understanding of a project close to their own research. This type of question requires a more detailed answer.

For example

I'm very keen on what you say about the distance from the highest to the lowest place on the earth. How is it being carried out in your laboratory?

I'm very much interested in hearing your presentation today on the Scientific Assumptions since the work we're going to start has some connections with yours. Now, would you please say a few more words about the tentative assumption? Particularly at its preliminary stage?

(3) Questions for raising different opinions.

Scientific research tends to lead to different conclusions, opinions or viewpoints. Therefore, it is quite natural to find different opinions in professional discussion sessions. For example,

The last point you mentioned is something related to the subject we've been studying. I'd say I've got some insights from your views. But as to your saying about... I'm afraid that at least the following case seems to have been overlooked. The first point...The second point... And the last point... Can I have your comments on that?

(4) Questions for comprehensive examinations.

Sometimes in the discussion sessions, several questions raised by one person move step by step for further investigation and have internal relationships. Such questions could usually be seen in the oral defense of theses or interviews. For example,

Thank you very much for your detailed explanation. But I still have a few more questions. Do you think this process can be industrialized? If so, when will it be industrialized? Do you think this method can completely take the place of other pollutant treatment methods? Why did you put forward that plan? How did you think of the idea? Were there any difficulties in performing the resolution? And how did you overcome the difficulties, if any?

A series of questions are raised in order to make a full investigation of all the aspects, to obtain a systematic description of the topic, and to lead the speaker to the desired answer step by step. By way of asking a series of questions related to the subject, the presenter's comprehension and ability can be comprehensively examined. That's why such questions are often heard in the oral defense of theses, dissertations or interviews.

(5) Questions for information-hunting

As is known to all, an international academic conference serves both as a place for displaying research accomplishments, and as a place for exchanging information. Therefore, at a professional meeting, especially at a scientific and technological conference naturally exists the problem of how to completely lay bare the latest knowledge on the one hand and appropriately avoid disclosing the sensitive information on the other hand. Therefore, some of the audience might raise questions with the purpose of collecting information about detailed data, specimens, examples, specific technologies, etc. For example:

● Thank you very much for your patient explanation in response to my question. But I have one more question, or rather a request—can I have a copy of your report on the gyroscope(陀螺仪)? I'm interested in its industrial applications.

● I have heard about your study on atmospheric propagation, I'd like to know how many ground stations there are in our country and in your city as well.

● By the way, do you happen to know about the controversial subject of genetics, which was presented at the previous session?

2. Possible answers to different questions

Although answering questions does not take long during oral defense, it reflects the speaker's special knowledge, language proficiency, strategy employment, and relative experience, etc. Due to the unpredictable situations and different understandings of individuals, it is either impractical or impossible to set rules for what to do or what to say under certain circumstances. Our discussion is centered on the general principles of answers to different questions. The examples given are just a small part of the rich language data. In the following description, we'll discuss the principles of answering questions with suggestive answers to the questions under the heading of ordinary questions, questions of disagreement, noncommittal questions and rebuking questions.

(1) To ordinary questions.

The so-called ordinary questions mean the type of questions asked by the audience who do not quite catch a point and who have special interests. These questions normally call for clear elaboration and explanation. To answer them requires the speaker to give concise and explicit repetition, description, verification or correction. For example:

Q: I don't quite understand what you really mean by saying "…" Can you explain it again?

A: To answer your question, I'd like to repeat the third point of what I said just now. Well, I was saying…

To answer this type of question, the speaker usually should give a "whole" speech. His response should have three steps: repetition of the question, answering the question, and reassurance. Even though the speaker may be offering an impromptu speech, he is expected to structure ideas and information clearly and rationally. A typical pattern for an elaborated remark might like this:

• Repetition of the question: a rephrasing of the question to clarify it for the other listeners; an indication of why the question is a good one; a forecast of the steps you will take in answering it.

• Answering the question: offering the information or explanation called for.

• Reassurance: a direct reference to the person asking the question to see if further elaboration or explanation is needed, as in the examples above.

(2) To questions of disagreement.

When answering questions of disagreement to some presented opinions, ideas, and viewpoints, the speaker should follow the principles of respecting facts to explain his ideas and persuade the questioner with reason. Meanwhile, he should have a sincere attitude and avoid stubbornness. For example:

Q: Perhaps we're looking at the problem from different viewpoints. To the best of my knowledge, what you say seems to be theoretically unclear in... For example, ... Could you give us a further explanation about that aspect?

A: Well, judging from your question, I can see that your understanding of my viewpoints seems to be somewhat different from my original intention. That awkwardness was due to the so short time that I couldn't put it clearly. Here I'd like to explain it briefly. My original intention is ...

Q: I am of the opinion that the subject is well set forth, and the approaches to solving the problem are also reasonable. But so far ...is concerned, I am afraid I can't say that I go along with you on that. Because ... And I'd like to turn all my ears to you on that.

A: I'm afraid that our different views on the point may come from the different angles from which we're looking at the problem. My idea is mainly out of the theoretical considerations, specifically on the basis of the following three aspects: the first point is...

(3) To noncommittal questions.

Noncommittal questions refer to those sensitive questions that are inappropriate to answer directly. Generally speaking, participants tend to seek as much useful information as possible especially about some particular data, samples, examples and applied technology. Therefore, a careful attitude should be taken in answering this type of questions. The answer should be brief, reserved, and flexible. As for questions that are time-consuming or are inconvenient to answer, it should be explained, inferred, or shifted to another topic, while evasive inquiry questions should be evaded. The following are some examples of the answers to the questions, to which it would be inappropriate to give direct answers. For example:

Q: (A question raised to know the technical details)

A: ...I believe that you've put forward a good question. You're perfectly right here by saying that the project promises a wide application in industry. But so far as the technological process of its manufacturing is concerned, I'm afraid it's too involved to be treated with one word or two. You may find the newly published book entitled Gyroscope, and go over the fourth chapter which deals with the configuration and fabrication of the gyroscope. Besides, we may also make an appointment to exchange our views on the subject if it's convenient for you ...

3. Techniques for answering

In a question-and-answer session (especially in an oral defense), an answerer should be quick in thinking and expressing ideas. On the one hand, the answerer should organize the answer in a flexible way according to the nature of the question; on the other hand, he should think over the answer on his own so as not to be controlled by the question-raisers, and should take the initiative. Thus, attention should be paid to the following aspects:

(1) Hearing the question clearly.

Attentively catching the question forms the basis of answering, without which the answerer might give an apparently right but actually wrong answer, or answer what is not asked. Nothing is more frustrating to a questioner than an answer that misses the point or drifts into territory irrelevant to the query. There are many ways to confirm the question raised, or rather, to ask the question-raiser to repeat the question. For example:

Pardon? (Beg your pardon? I beg your pardon? Sorry, I am sorry ...)

What was that (the last word, the last sentence), please?

Sorry, I didn't catch (follow, understand, get, etc.) what you've said. Would you mind repeating (telling me) your question again?

(2) Judging correctly the question.

Some questions have meanings beyond the words, i.e., the real intention of a question differs from the literal meaning. In this case, not only the literal meaning should be clearly understood, but also the real motivation, attitude, and connotation 2 should be noticed as well. Let's look at the following questions.

Could you please tell us the essential difference between your experimental-design and that of Professor Baker's?

In the above example, the questioner by the question might doubt the originality of the speaker's experimental design. Therefore, mere literal understanding and answering may not have the desired effect. Sometimes, the content of a question entails a kind of premise, for example:

Are you still going on building the ground stations?

This question may help obtain information about the establishment of ground stations.

An answer of either "Yes" or "No" is dangerous. If the answerer says "Yes", it is meant that he has been building ground stations; while "No" will show that he built ground stations before. Only when the answerer has made a correct inference of the question, can he give an appropriate answer like the following one, for example:

"We have never built any ground stations."

(3) Copying the original question pattern.

Sometimes, the information contained in a question can be used to guide the orientation of the answer and thus makes the answer more tactful. For example:

Question: If you failed in your experiment, would you think that all your previous efforts were wasted?

Answer: If I failed in my experiment, I would not think that my previous efforts were wasted, for a scientific experiment failure itself tells us the result.

Question: (In a less-than-friendly way) If you don't mind, I would frankly ask you a question.

Answer: I'm afraid you have made a number of faulty assumptions in your presentation ... (Aware of the ill intention) If you don't mind, I will frankly answer your question. I'm afraid you have made a series of false charges in your question ...

Question: Is there any difference between the description in your manuscript and the presentation in your speech just now?

Answer: Yes, there is. The difference is that one is written and another is spoken.

(4) Repeating the previous remarks.

The content of the presentation forms the foundation of the oral defense. If a speaker is good at citing the content of the previous presentation, it will be helpful for him to answer the questions. This kind of citation has the following two advantages:

- It helps the speaker overcome his nervousness and create confidence so as to offer a reasonable, fluent, and natural answer.

Unit 4 International Conference

● It makes the answer consistent and cohesive. The original facts, specific data, figures and tables make the answer more convincing. Frequently adopted expressions in citing previous remarks are as follows:

To answer your question, I will just repeat what I said in my talk...

Concerning this point, I think I have touched on it in my speech...

If you are interested in that detailed parameters, I would suggest you look them up in my manuscript on page seven, which have been shown in my presentation.

Useful Expressions and Sentence Patterns

Expressions for the questioner

1. To make a self-introduction（自我介绍）

(1) My name is Maria Schiff, and I work for the State of Massachusetts.

(2) I'm George Greenberg, and I work at the Department of Health and Hunan Services.

(3) My name is Gary Lindsey. I'm with Partnership for Prevention in Washington.

(4) I'm Sean Gallagher from NIOSH.

2. To raise questions or make comments（提问或评价）

(1) You did touch a bit on it in the second half, but my question was about if this new technology could be universally applied.

(2) Thinking about actually other areas, my question is in regard to the extent that Wall Street has looked at other areas, particularly the impact on productivity.

(3) I wonder, is there any standard for evidence coming from these other /entities, like tribunals, World Court, that kind of thing?

(4) This is part observation and perhaps partly a question to consider and it builds on what's just been said. I'm wondering how we can build a consciousness, an awareness, amongst the people who are producing this material and preserving it.

(5) Mr. Sherman, I am wondering what your thoughts are on the price of music to the public.

(6) I have two questions and they're for Bill Marras. I enjoyed your presentation and the multimedia associated with it. The first question is the problems that I've

seen in the warehouse industry have a lot to do with timing issues and time standards. And I was wondering whether or not you had addressed that portion of the research?

(7) I wanted to thank all of you for your presentations. They were excellent, but the question I have for you, Dan, is relative to these task teams.

Expressions for the speaker

1. To make the question clear（确认提问）

(1) Can you speak a little more distinctly? I'm having a little trouble understanding.

(2) Are we talking about the people actually using the ship?

(3) I'm sorry. I didn't hear you clearly. What's your last point, please?

(4) I don't quite follow what you were saying. Would you please repeat what you just said?

(5) I'm afraid I don't really understand what you are getting at.

2. To make comments on the question（对问题进行评价）

(1) I think that's a great question.

(2) This is an excellent question that raises several important issues.

(3) What you are asking is a key question.

(4) That's an interesting question.

(5) A good question.

3. To express agreements or disagreements（表示同意或不同意）

(1) Absolutely.

(2) Exactly.

(3) I totally agree with you.

(4) I'm in complete agreement with you.

(5) Well, I disagree.

(6) I'm afraid I have to disagree with you.

4. To handle difficult or irrelevant questions（应对难题或无关的问题）

(1) I'm afraid I can't answer that question.

(2) I think it will be possible to answer your question when this experiment is completed.

(3) The answer to your question needs further study.

(4) Would you mind if I dealt with that question later?

(5) I'm sorry to tell you that I don't have that kind of information.

(6) Professor Wood perhaps is in a better position to tell us something about it.

5. To ask whether the answer given is satisfactory（询问回答是否满意）

(1) Are you satisfied with the answer?

(2) This is my answer. Is it enough for your question?

(3) Did that answer your question?

(4) I hope this answered your question.

Tips for Answering Questions

- If you do not know the answer to a question, admit it. At the beginning of your presentation, tell the audience about your level, experience, and point of view. Then you can answer "that's out of my area." However, do offer to find out the answer and tell the person later.

- Repeat the question in a large group or arrange for microphones, so others can hear the question. Talk to the entire audience, not just the person asking the question.

- Make sure you understand the question. Some people indirectly ask their real question.

- Angry questions do not have to be answered. Answer personal, angry or unrelated questions with "see me after."

- Do not let an interesting but unrelated question start you on a new speech. Keep your answers short.

- Allow Q&A time if you said there would be questions. Do not continue your presentation thinking that the Q&A time is extra time for your presentation.

- When the time for questions is finished, announce one more question and suggest "see me after" for others after that.

- Consider questions as an honor to you and your presentation. Good ideas create questions. Boring presentations make people leave.

Unit 5

Practical Writings

Learning Objectives

In this unit, you will learn to accomplish the following tasks:

➢ Task 1: To familiarize the format of a letter of application
➢ Task 2: To prepare a cover letter
➢ Task 3: To write a curriculum vitae
➢ Task 4: To write a personal statement

Task 1: Letter of Application

General Introduction

1. What are letters of application?

The application letter is the first impression the selector will have of the candidate and its negative or positive impact is going to influence his or her further reading (or not) the CV or resume.

2. Format of letters of application

Letterhead
Date of writing
Inside address
Salutation
Body of the letter
- How you got the advertisement, purpose of the letter/reasons for your choice, position name
- A brief self-introduction: general information, your education, academic area(s)/interest, research work
  - Working experiences
  - Other related qualifications/skills
  - Requesting information, financial support
  - Contact information

Complimentary close
Signature
Enclosure/Postscript/Copies (if any)

3. Tips

In order to write a strong letter of application, it is important for you to follow the following tips:
- Make use of business letter format

If you want to make such letters effective, then make use of the business letter format. Friendly letter format is strictly not allowed. In the business letter format, you should always add contact information at the top. Don't forget to add salutation at the beginning and signature at the end.

- Mention your skills and abilities

Understand that in such a letter, you are selling yourself. So it is important to mention your skills and abilities in detail but without exaggerating. See to it that the skills you mention can benefit the company. If required, you can also add numerical values to your accomplishments.

- Make use of key phrases or keywords

Have you read the job listing carefully? If yes, then circle the important phrases mentioned in the job listing. Use those phrases in your application letter in order to create a good impact on an employer.

- Write a concise letter

It is important to write a concise letter because the employer will not be interested in reading a long letter. Your letter should not include more than four paragraphs.

- Editing is important

Don't just submit your letter without proofreading it. It is important to edit in order to avoid any kind of errors. Editing can allow you to get rid of grammar and spelling errors.

Sample Demonstration

Sample 1: Applying Letter for a Job

Flat K, 30/F
Block 5, Fulrich Villa
Shatin, H.K.
January 14, 2010

Mr. Tony Lee
Personnel Manager
Thomas Green Ltd.

Rm. 383, Bldg. Hang Fung
112-114 Rd. Prince
Kowloon, H.K.

Dear Mr. Lee,

    With reference to the advertisement in the ABC on January 11, 2010, I am writing to apply for the position of Computer Graphic Designer.

    I am currently a full-time student studying a degree course in Information Technology at the Hong Kong Polytechnic University and I am due to graduate in June 2010. As you can see from the enclosed CV, I have extensive experience in computer graphic design. Apart from the formal training I have obtained from my three-year course and summer programs, I have had a number of part-time and summer jobs which have helped me to gain experience in designing computer graphics. Frequent participation in workshops, competitions and extra-curricular activities involving the subject has also allowed me to develop insight into the area.

    My professional training at the university requires adaptability and creative use of the resources available to produce graphics for real customers in the business world. Working as a student researcher during the last semester has further expanded my skills in data processing and graphic design, and more importantly, my ability to work independently. I feel, therefore, that I have not only the experience that you are looking for but a number of other invaluable skills which would benefit me in this position.

    I would like to have the opportunity to discuss this position with you further. I can be contacted at 67868888 or 13912345678 between 8:30 am and 6:30 pm. Thank you for your consideration and I await your reply.

                                                            Yours Sincerely,
                                                                Li Yu

Encl. CV

Sample 2: Application Letter for a Ph.D. Program

School of Chemistry and Chemical Engineer

Shandong University

27 Shanda Nanlu

Jinan 250110,

P. R. China

May 22, 2014

Office of Admissions

Michigan State University

250 Hannah Administration Building

East Lansing, Michigan 48824-0509

USA

Dear Office of Admissions,

I am a student in the School of Chemistry and Chemical Engineer at Shandong University. I am expecting to get my master's degree in July next year. I am very interested in pursuing a Ph.D. degree in Chemistry at the Natural Science Department of Michigan State University. I find that Michigan State University has a long history and a good academic atmosphere. That is my ideal school. I intend to enter in the autumn of 2015.

In recent years, I have worked hard. You can see from my curriculum vitae. I have remained top 5% of about 100 students. I also worked with Professor Shi Laishun on research topics like Chlorine dioxide oscillation reaction. I know that there are professors doing related research in your school. I hope I can have a chance for further study. In addition, I am well prepared linguistically for the study in the US. My TOEFL is 620 and my GRE is 1300.

I would be grateful if you would send me the application forms for admission and financial support at your early convenience. Thank you for your consideration.

I am looking forward to hearing from you soon.

Sincerely yours,

Chen Jingjing

Useful Expressions

1. Openings

(1) I am a researcher at the Experimental Center of Medical Molecular Biology at Shandong University. Prof. Li Lin recommended that I get in touch with you about membership in your working group.

(2) I have learned from Prof. Melba Ripley of the University of Louisiana that you are the Secretary of the Translators Association. In this connection, I would like to know whether I am eligible for membership in your association.

(3) I am a Ph. D. candidate at the School of Materials Engineering at Purdue University. I am very delighted to learn from my friend, William Wade, Associate Director of the Center for Asian and Pacific Studies, that you would like to have visiting scholars for the 2007-2008 academic year.

(4) Prof. Li Lin of Jiaotong University, P. R. China, who was a visiting scholar in your Department of Business Studies 2003-2004, advised me of the outstanding MBA program in your university.

2. Purpose

(1) I am writing to you to apply for admittance to your university as a visiting scholar.

(2) I am writing to you about the possibility of attending the forthcoming conference.

(3) I wish to learn about construction techniques for developing new structures in your working group for six months, preferably during April through September.

(4) I wish to attend the American Translators Association 48th annual Conference to be held for October 31 to November 3, 2007, in San Francisco, California.

(5) I am writing to inquire about applying for membership in your Center for Economic Research.

(6) I am deeply interested in your Ph. D. program in information and electrical engineering at your graduate school and plan to apply for admission for the fall of 2007.

3. Research interests/areas

(1) My own work combines research, primarily in contemporary British drama, with the dramaturgical development of new plays. I also have an ongoing interest in contemporary American drama, which makes me actively involved as a dramaturge with new play development.

(2) My research is concerned primarily with the origin of barriers to gene exchange, especially the evolutionary genetics of reproductive isolation.

(3) My research interests include moral, pedagogical and cultural writings, extending through three ideological traditions in English and American literature, imaginative writing and professional writing. My current focus is the referential relationship between language and writing.

4. Research work

(1) Currently, I am involved in a long-term program entitled WTO and Economic Positions of the Developing Countries.

(2) I have been undertaking research on biomedical signal processing for two years.

(3) In my work, I have focused especially on optoelectronic materials.

(4) I have been carrying on this work since I started my Ph. D. program.

(5) I have been engaged in the energy conservation project for more than two years.

(6) I am a researcher at the School of Materials Engineering of Purdue University. I have devoted nearly five years to the study of how inexpensive housing can be made of native materials in Third World countries.

(7) I am a biomedical engineer with five years of experience in designing nonintrusive methods for diagnosing a variety of medical conditions.

5. Expectation of academic exchange

(1) I believe that attending such a conference will provide me with a very good opportunity to exchange ideas and expertise with attendees from different parts of the world and, more importantly, to learn from them.

(2) I hope it will be possible for me to take such courses as materials science and to work in your laboratory during my visit to your university. I believe that with

your help I will make progress in my specialty.

(3) We are enthusiastic about continuing our exchange agreement with your laboratory and finalizing in the near future the details of the next five-year plan between our two laboratories.

(4) Attending the conference will broaden my horizons.

6. Desired/Intended time of entry

(1) I wish to participate in your working group for six months, preferably during April through September.

(2) I intend to enter in the fall of 2007.

(3) My desired time of entrance is fall 2008.

7. Financial support

(1) Our institute will provide me with all traveling and living expenses.

(2) If possible, I wish to obtain a scholarship so that I may support myself and obtain some teaching experience while pursuing graduate studies.

(3) I have sufficient financial resources to cover my educational expenses, so I shall not seek financial support in any form from your institute.

8. Requesting information/materials

(1) I would appreciate it if you could send me the application forms for admission and financial aid/support.

(2) I would be grateful if you could send me any further information pertinent to the forthcoming conference.

(3) I would be very much obliged if you could send me the application forms and details concerning financial aid.

(4) Would you be kind to furnish me with some related information?

(5) I would be grateful if you would forward me the necessary materials and relevant information about the research project at your earliest convenience.

9. Supplying information

(1) If you need any additional information, please do not hesitate to contact me.

(2) If further materials are required, I am willing to forward them to you.

10. Enclosure(s)

(1) Enclosed please find a copy of my curriculum vitae/resume, a photo of my academic degree certificate, and two photographs.

(2) I am enclosing my curriculum vitae, together with my photographs.

(3) You will find enclosed a photocopy of my ID card, a photograph of my university diploma, and a photocopy of my technical qualification certificate.

(4) Please refer to my enclosed CV for details.

Task 2: Cover Letters

⧗ General Introduction

1. What are cover letters?

Cover Letters are letters sent along with other documents to provide additional information. They can be sent along with application letters or with the paper submitted to the scientific journal.

2. Types of cover letters

(1) The original manuscript.
(2) Reminder letter.
(3) Revised manuscript.
(4) Response to the reviewer's comments.
(5) Thanks to the editor or the reviewer.
(6) Inquiry about proofs.
(7) Proofreading.

⧗ Sample Demonstration

1. The original manuscript

Dear Editors:

We would like to submit the enclosed manuscript entitled "Paper Title", which we wish to be considered for publication in "Journal Name". No conflict of interest exists in the submission of this manuscript, and the manuscript is approved by all authors for publication. I would like to declare on behalf of my co-authors that the work described was original research that has not been published previously, and not under consideration for publication elsewhere, in whole or in part. All the authors listed have approved the manuscript that is enclosed.

In this work, we evaluated …（简要介绍一下论文的创新性）I hope this paper is suitable for "Journal Name".

The following is a list of possible reviewers for your consideration:
1. Name A   E-mail: ××××@××××   2. Name B   E-mail: ××××@××××

We deeply appreciate your consideration of our manuscript, and we look forward to receiving comments from the reviewers. If you have any inquiries, please don't hesitate to contact me at the address below.

Thank you and best regards.

Yours sincerely,
××××××

Corresponding author:
Name: ×××
E-mail: ××××@××××

2. Reminder letter

Dear Prof. ×××:

Sorry for disturbing you. I am not sure if it is the right time to contact you to inquire about the status of my submitted manuscript titled "Paper Title". ID: 文章稿号, although the status of "With Editor" has been lasting for more than two months, since submitted to journal three months ago. I am just wondering whether my manuscript has been sent to reviewers or not. I would be greatly appreciated if you could spend some of your time checking the status for us. I am very pleased to hear from you on the reviewer's comments. Thank you very much for your consideration.

Best regards!

Yours sincerely,
××××××

Corresponding author:
Name: ×××
E-mail: ×××@××××

3. Revised manuscript

Dear Dr/ Prof.:

On behalf of my co-authors, we thank you very much for giving us an opportunity to revise our manuscript, we appreciate editor and reviewers very much for their positive and constructive comments and suggestions on our manuscript entitled "Paper Title". ID: 文章稿号.

We have studied the reviewer's comments carefully and have made revision which marked in red in the paper. We have tried our best to revise our manuscript according to the comments. Attached please find the revised version, which we would like to submit for your kind consideration. We would like to express our great appreciation to you and reviewers for comments on our paper. Looking forward to hearing from you. Thank you and best regards.

Yours sincerely,
××××××

Corresponding author:
Name: ×××
E-mail: ××××@××××

4. Response to the reviewer's comments

Dear Editors and Reviewers:

Thank you for your letter and for the reviewers' comments concerning our manuscript entitled "Paper Title" ID: 文章稿号. Those comments are all valuable and very helpful for revising and improving our paper, as well as the important guiding significance to our researches. We have studied comments carefully and have made correction which we hope meet with approval. Revised portions are marked in red in the paper. The main corrections in the paper and the response to the reviewer's comments are as follows:

Response to the reviewer's comments:

Reviewer #1:

1. Response to comment: … Response: ××××××
2. Response to comment: … Response: ××××××

We are very sorry for our negligence of... We are very sorry for our incorrect writing ... It is really true as reviewer suggested that ...

We have made correction according to the Reviewer's comments. We have re-written this part according to the Reviewer's suggestion. As Reviewer suggested that ... Considering the reviewer's suggestion, we have ...

Special thanks to you for your good comments.

Reviewer #2:　同上述
Reviewer #3:　同上述

Other changes:
1. Line 60-61, the statements of "..." were corrected as "..."
2. Line 107, "..." was added
3. Line 129, "..." was deleted

We tried our best to improve the manuscript and made some changes in the manuscript. These changes will not influence the content and framework of the paper. And here we did not list the changes but marked in red in the revised paper.

We appreciate the editors/reviewers' warm work earnestly and hope that the correction will meet with approval.

Once again, thank you very much for your comments and suggestions.

Yours sincerely,

(Signature)

Corresponding author:
Name: ×××
E-mail: ××××@××××

5. Thanks to the editor or the reviewer

Dear Prof. ×××××:

　　Thanks very much for your kind work and consideration on publication of our paper. On behalf of my co-authors, we would like to express our great appreciation to the editors and reviewers. Thank you and best regards.

Yours sincerely,
××××××

Corresponding author: .
Name: ×××
E-mail: ××××@××××

6. Inquiry about proofs

Dear×××:

　　Sorry for disturbing you. I am not sure if it is the right time to contact you to inquire about the status of our accepted manuscript titled "Paper Title" ID: 文章稿号, since the copyright agreement for publication has been sent to you for two months. I am just wondering how long I can receive the proof of our manuscript from you.

　　I would be greatly appreciated if you could spend some of your time on a reply. I am very pleased to hear from you.

　　Thank you very much for your consideration.

Yours sincerely,
××××××

Corresponding author:
Name: ×××
E-mail: ××××@××××

7. Proofreading

Dear Mr. ×××:

Thanks very much for your kind letter about the proof of our paper titled "Paper Title" ID: 文章稿号 for publication in "Journal Name". We have finished the proofreading and checking carefully, and some corrections about the proof and the answers to the inquiries are provided below.

Corrections:

1. In ****** should be **** Page ***, Right column, line***

2. In **** the "*****" should be "****" Page ****, Right column, line****

Answers for "author inqueries":

1. ********************. 2. ********************* 3. *********************

We greatly appreciate the efficient, professional and rapid processing of our paper by your team. If there is anything else we should do, please do not hesitate to let us know. Thank you and best regards.

Yours sincerely,

××××××

Corresponding author:

Name: ×××

E-mail: ××××@××××

Task 3: Curriculum Vitae (CV)

General Introduction

What is CV?

A curriculum vitae (CV) is a written overview of a person's experience and other qualifications. In some countries, a CV is typically the first item that a potential employer encounters regarding the job seeker and is typically used to screen applicants, often followed by an interview. A curriculum vitae, commonly referred to as CV, is a longer two or more pages, more detailed synopsis than a resume. It includes a summary of your educational and academic background, as well as teaching and research experience, publications, presentations, awards, honors, affiliations, and other details. When you compose your CV, try to give the information that will show you in the best possible light. If you are applying for an academic exchange program, you will enclose your CV for the experts' consideration.

Comparison between resume and CV

A resume is a brief written account of one's personal details. When we are applying for a job, we usually send a resume together with our letter of application. A CV is more detailed in content.

Format of CV

(1) Personal details optional: date of birth, place of birth, nationality, marital status.

(2) Name, affiliation, phone, email address.

(3) Education background.

(4) Research areas/interests, current research projects, work in progress.

(5) Teaching experience.

(6) Selected publications, conference presentations.

(7) Honors and awards.

(8) Professional membership.

(9) Other information.

Tips for Writing a CV

- Identification

Begin the CV with your name, centered at the top of the page; your affiliation, address, phone number and email address directly underneath or on the right.

- Objective optional

Put the objective at the top of the CV after your address, making sure it is precise.

How to Describe Your Objective?

- Certain personal quality and capability for the vacancy.
- To the point.
- Use phrases rather than complete sentences.
- Use action verbs to describe your achievements.
- Use parallel structures.
- Make the CV reader-friendly.
- Try to be error-free.

Sample Demonstration

Sample 1: A Resume Sample

Name: Ellen Wang

Address: 4000 Smith Avenue, Minneapolis,
    MN, USA 55404

Date of Birth: March 7, 1975

Sex: Female

Marital status: Single

Health: Excellent
Education
    1996–1998   No.2 Middle School, Beijing, China
    1998–2002   Citrus Community College, California
                     Major: TESL
                     Received B.A. in English, July 2002
    2002–2004   Mt. San Antonio College, Walnut, California
                     Major: Linguistics
                     Received M.A. in March 2004.
Work Experience
    Summer 2001 Assistant Secretary, Sunflower Co. Ltd. Glendora, California
    2002–2004   English Tutor, Mt. San. Antonio High School, Walnut, California
    1996   Translator and Interpreter, Australian Aid Roc. Company, Tianjin Branch
    1997-present Teacher of English Tianjin Institute of Finance and Trade Administration
Awards and Honors
    2001   National Merit Scholarship Award
    2002–2004   Mt. San. Antonio College Honor Roll
    2002   Bank of America English Achievement Award
Membership
    1998–2004   Member of California Scholarship Federation
                     Interests Travel, swimming, playing guitar
References   Available upon request

Sample 2: A CV Sample

Allen Yan

861338-1111-420

yhnasa@123.com

EDUCATION

Sep 2002–Present, Shanghai University, BE

- Candidate for Bachelor in Mechanical Engineering degree ME.
- Major academic courses: Company Property Management; Marketing; Economics; English
- Technology Communication; Information Management System; Modern Fabrication System; Certified Public Accounting Training CPA May 2006

OCCUPATION

Dec 2005–present, ITT Flygt investment. China

Application Engineer, Sales & Marketing

- Application support and industry projects tracing to the sales office to achieve the sales budget and new industry market application research.
- Pay suitable visits to end users and DI for seminars and technical presentations with salesperson or distributors while collect marketing information and competitor information analysis.

July 2005–Sep 2005, Intel Products Co., Shanghai, China

CPU Assembly Engineer Internship

- Analyzed the yield ratio trend, documented and solved the current problems.
- Participated in the training of marketing, business process modeling and analysis at Intel University.
- Visualized a project review with impressive presentation and multi-media animation, which was highly appreciated by the department manager.

June 2005–July 2005, GF Fund Management Co., LTD.

Campus Intern

- Analyzed investment principles and mischoose of related financial derived products.
- Formulated the scheme of market popularization and network marketing.

AWARDS

- 2004–2005, the Imagine Ambassador of Shanghai Tennis Popularization.
- 2003–2004, Second-Class Scholarship for Excellent Students of Shanghai University.

COMPETENCIES & INTERESTS

- English Ability: Band 6 and the intermediate test of interpretation.
- Germany Ability: 600 hours of Germany lessons at Tongji University.

Computer Skills:

- National Computer Level 3rd Certificate. Network Communication
- Professional Certificate of Assistant Information Officer AIO.

Membership

- National Council Teachers of English
- Alliance of Computers and Composition
- Rhetoric Society of America

Personal Interests:

Basketball: skilled; Skating: speed; English: elegant; Snooker: stable

Sample 3

Curriculum Vitae

Yeon-Koo Che

February 2009

ADDRESS

Department of Economics

Columbia University

420 West 118th Street, Rm 1016 IAB

New York, NY 10027

Phone: 212-854-8276; Fax: 212-854-8059.

E-mail: yc2271@columbia.edu

Home Page: http://www.columbia.edu/~yc2271

EDUCATION

Stanford University, Ph.D., 1991 Advisor: Paul Milgrom

University of Toronto, M.A., 1986

Seoul National University, B. Econ., 1984

EMPLOYMENT

Professor, Columbia University, 2005-

Professor, University of Wisconsin, 2000-2006;

Associate Professor, University of Wisconsin, 1997-2000;

Visiting Professor, Institut d' Analisi Economica, Barcelona, Spain, 1998-1999;

John M. Olin Faculty Fellow, the Yale Law School, 1996;

Assistant Professor, University of Wisconsin, 1991-1997;

Consultant, RAND Corporation, 1989 Summer.

EDITORIAL POSITIONS

Editor: Journal of Industrial Economics 2003- ;

Associate Editor: Journal of Economic Theory 2008- ;

Associate Editor: Theoretical Economics 2005- ;

Co-Editor: Journal of Economics and Management Strategy 1999-2003 ;

Associate Editor: Journal of Industrial Economics 2002-2003;

Editorial Board: International Economic Journal 1999- ;

Editorial Board: Korean Economic Review 2005- .

GRANTS

National Science Foundation Grant, on "Market Design" PI, 2007-2010.

National Science Foundation Grant, on "Holdup" PI, 2003-2005.

PUBLICATION Refereed Journals

"Optimal Collusion-Proof Auctions," with Jinwoo Kim, Journal of Economic Theory, 2009, 144, 565-603.

"Strategic Judgment Proofing," with Kathryn Spier, Rand Journal of Economics, 2008, 39, 926-48

"Exploiting Plaintiffs Through Settlement: Divide and Conquer," with Kathryn Spier, Journal of Institutional and Theoretical Economics, 2008, 164, 4-23.

RESEARCH IN PROGRESS

"Opinions as Incentives," with Navin Kartik, revised and resubmit, Journal of Political Economy.

"Bidding with Securities: Comment," with Jinwoo Kim, revised and resubmit, American Economic Review.

"Market versus Non-Market Assignment of Ownership," with Ian Gale, submitted.

AWARDS AND HONOR

KAEA-Maekyung Economist Award, KAEA; Maekyung Daily, 2009;

Cho Rakkyo Award, Yonsei University, 2008 inaugural recipient;

Shoemaker Fellow, UW-Madison, 2004-2005;

Mary Claire Phipps Fellow, UW-Madison, 2004-2005;

H.I. Romnes Prize, UW-Madison, 1999;

John M. Olin Faculty Fellowship, Yale Law School, 1996;

Lynde and Harry Bradley Fellowship, Stanford University, 1990

PROFESSIONAL ACTIVITIES

The 17th Jerusalem Summer School in Economics Theory: Invited Lecturer, 2006.

Econometric Society: Program Committee for the Far Eastern Meeting 2003.

International Summer School Invited Lecturer Oberwesel, Germany, 2000.

John M Olin Invited Lecturer USC Law School, 1999.

TEACHING

Graduate Courses:

　　Industrial Organization Theory

　　Microeconomic Theory

　　Topics in Microeconomic Theory

Undergraduate Courses:

　　Law and Economics

　　Game Theory

Intermediate Microeconomics

RECENT SEMINAR

2008:

Princeton University Institute for Advanced Studies

Yonsei University Cho Award Lecture

Korean Econometric Society Meeting Invited Session

Association for Public Economic Theory Conference

2007:

Berkeley Law School

Stanford University

Harvard Market Design Workshop

Brown University

Duke University

Paris School of Economics

University of Hong Kong Mini-Conference on Micro Theory

STUDENTS ADVISED

Principal advisor: Kazumi Hori Hitotsubashi University, Japan, 2005,

Jinwoo Kim USC, 2003,

Yasu Tamada Keio University, Japan, 2002,

Kyoungwon RheeKISDI, Korea, 2000.

Dissertation Committee: Changxiu Sue Li Lehman Brothers,

Unjy Song UBC,

Ming Li Concordia University,

Cheng-Tai Wu National Chengchi University, Taiwan

Useful Expressions

1. Useful glossary for personality

able, active, adaptable, ambitious, analytical, aspiring, capable, careful, competent, confident, constructive, cooperative, creative, dedicated, diplomatic, disciplined, dutiful/responsible, dynamic, diligent, effective, efficient, energetic, enthusiastic, extrovert/introvert, faithful, frank, friendly, generous, gentle, hard-working, honest, humorous, independent, initiative, intelligent, knowledgeable, logical, loyal, objective, motivated, open-minded, original, practical, punctual, qualified, reasonable, reliable, self-conscious, sincere, smart, strict, strong-willed

2. Useful expressions and sentence patterns

Education

B.A. in English Language and literature, College of Foreign Languages, Beijing University

M.S. in Chemical Engineering, Department of Chemistry, Sichuan University

M.S. Candidate in Computer Science and Technology, Nankai University

Ph. D in physics, University of Melbourne, Australia

Curriculum

Major courses concerning Management including: Accounting, Management, Marketing, Economics, Statistics, Business Education, etc

Courses completed: Monetary Banking, 88; Insurance, 92; Marketing, 90; Project Appraisal, 88; International Finance, 91; International Settlement, 87

Accounting courses including: Management Accounting, EDP Accounting, Cost Accounting, Industrial Accounting, Corporate Finance, Financial Statement Analysis

Objective

Researcher on Applied Linguistics at the postdoctoral level

A lecturer of law at Tianjin University

Work History

International Loan Section. Responsible for housing loans and for working assistant to the manager of the accounting department in a joint venture enterprise

Work experience in personnel affairs in a foreign-funded enterprise, coupled with an educational background in personnel management

Office Director Responsibilities with this construction company were primarily supervisory

Directed a staff of 38 in bookkeeping, payroll and drafting departments

Served as an Advertising Designer for the Shanghai Art Service Agency

Academic Work History

1992-1994 Lecturer, Department of Genetics, University of Leeds

1999-2006 Professor of Biology, School of Biology, University of Leeds

2006 Senior Research Fellow, Department of Physics, National University of Singapore

Conference Presentations

"The Promise and Peril of Teaching Technical Writing", Computers and Writing Conference, Gainesville FL, March 2004

"Who's Being Served?: Using Syllawebs", Computers and Writing Conference, Honolulu, Hawaii, May 2000

"What We're Doing in College Composition" panel, Illinois Association of Teachers of English, Itasca, IL, October 1995

"The Desire for Music: Enlightenment Ideals in Mozart's Don Giovanni", International Comparative Literature Association, Venice, Italy, September 25, 2005

Research Interests/Areas

Composition and Rhetorical Theory, Cultural Criticism, Computer-Mediated Communication, and Pedagogical Theory and Practices

American literature, practical writing for business English

Labor markets, the organization of work, social and economic policy on employment and unemployment

Certificates and Exams

Language Proficiency: College English Test Band Six

Technical Qualification Received Lecturer of Mathematics Certificate in 2002

Scored 627 in TOFEL in October 2003 and 2100 in GRE in February 2004

Teaching Experience

Taught three courses: Modern Chinese Literature, English Writing, and Chinese-English Translation

Academic Writing: The Modern World, Environmental Studies

Contemporary Poetry, Opera, Aesthetics

Statistics in Social Research

Quantitative Data Analysis

Honors and Awards

First prize winner of the 3rd Computer Program Designer Contest 2006

Scholarship of Advanced English Learner, Hebei Normal University 2003

Excellent Student from Guanghua Fund, Zhengzhou University in 2003

Member of the University Volleyball Team, contributed to the winning of the Nanjing College Students Volleyball Contest 2005

Summer Research Fellowship, English Department, University of Connecticut, 1993

Outstanding Dissertation Award, National Association for Research in Science Teaching 1995

Australian Postgraduate Research Award, 1982-1985

Major Grants

$289,440 grant PI to develop and launch a new academic minor at UNC Chapel Hill on Christianity and Culture, from John Templeton Foundation, August1, 2007-December 31, 2007

$3,960,000 grant PI on "The Religious Practices of American Youth", from Lilly Endowment Inc., August 1, 2001- July 31, 2005

Integrating Instructional Technology into Elementary Science Methods EDDV 341. Funded by Grants for the Improvement of Instruction: Technology, Center for Teaching Effectiveness, University of Delaware, Academic Year 1996-1997

Publications

Dissertation for Master's Degree: Influence of Psychological Factors upon Utterance

Papers: On Macro-modulation in the Socialist Market Economy", the 6th issue of Economics Studies, 2000

Publication: English Readings for CET Band Four. Wuhan University Publishing House, 1996

"The Teaching of Literature in Illinois Schools." Co-author with Tetesa Faulkner. Illinois English Bulletin, winter 1999

Professional Membership

Vice-president, Materials Research Society MRS since 2000

Member of the Society of Technical Communication

Member of the Swiss Association of Translators and Interpreters, and of the European Society for Translation

References

References: Will be furnished upon request.

References: To be supplied upon request.

References: All references available on request.

Task 4: Personal Statement

General Introduction

What is Personal Statement?

A personal statement, as a component of the application, is a statement introducing yourself to a committee/institution, it is used to supplement the information presented in the application with specific examples and convincing facts. More importantly, it aids the committee/institution to learn more about you so as to offer you a place or a fellowship/award in preference to your competitors. This statement often centers on your interests in the particular program or position, your personal background, the reasons for doing the graduate work, and your goals. The committee/institution will welcome any factors you wish to bring to its attention concerning your academic and work experience to date.

Format of Personal Statement

(1) Your purpose/interest in the particular program/position

(2) Background information supporting your interest or purpose: academic qualifications, previous research experience, current research interests, other relative experience

(3) Career goals

(4) The reasons why you want to join a certain institution/university

(5) Restaurant of your interest or goal optional

Tips

Do's:

- Demonstrate your considerable dedication to earn a master's and even a doctorate degree.

- Clearly state your reasons to choose a particular school.
- Have someone else proofread your essay.

Don'ts:
- Bring up topics to a prospective admissions committee.
- Use excessive words on your extracurricular activities.
- Reuse the same statement of purpose for each school you apply to.

Sample Demonstration

Sample 1 Personal Statement for Accounting and Finance

Since studying Business at GCSE level and Economics at AS level, I have developed an interest in the role of finance within businesses. Alongside my studies at school, I have also taken inspiration from my involvement in my father's part-time business. I have helped deal with some financial aspects of this business, including banking and completing annual accounts, from which I have developed several skills in working with figures and the ability to accurately handle, organize and analyze information. From this experience, I am intrigued to learn more about finance and accounting.

Currently, I am studying A levels in Psychology, Geography, and English Literature. I chose not to continue Economics to A2 level as the specific aspects of my other courses were much more relevant to my personal interests. Each of these subjects has given me valuable knowledge and understanding which I can apply to many other general areas. Studying Psychology has given me an insight into behaviors and attitudes in everyday involvement with people, both relatives and friends, as well as within society in general. The human aspects of my Geography course have provided me with the ability to better understand important issues on a global scale. In studying literature I have learned to communicate ideas more clearly and confidently, both in speech and in writing.

Outside of school, I enjoy reading both fiction books, mostly classic novels, mysteries, science fiction, fantasy, and non-fiction texts, generally including information about natural history and the economy. I read every day as this is something that I find beneficial to improve my general knowledge and provides me with an opportunity to spend some time on my own. In addition to this, I have an enthusiasm for computing. I am familiar with using spreadsheets, word processors and creative software and I am also learning aspects of web design. In recent years I have learned skills from my brother, who is a computer programmer, and I am always eager to teach myself new things.

As an individual, I have always aspired to higher education at university as I have a positive and committed attitude to learning new things. The idea of moving on from school life and taking on the challenge of a degree course provides me with motivation and determination to succeed. From studying at university, I intend to develop my personal characteristics and skills and learn to apply the knowledge I gain to pursue a career in an accounting or financial profession.

Sample 2   Personal Statement for an Academic Exchange Program

Graduating two years later with a B.S. in Physics Curriculum and Teaching Theory, I am especially interested in attending the State University of Michigan for exchange both for the theoretical knowledge and practical skills in a higher level in this field. My main interest, among the concentration of your exchange program of physics, is in science education.

I have always been a top student in my specialized area, physics. I took several other courses in my spare time and excelled in all of them due to my hard work. I am eager to further continue my study and constantly enrich the academic knowledge to broaden my horizons, know more teachers and classmates from departments of physics of different universities. Therefore, I treasure the opportunity of exchange at Michigan State University to accept various academic atmosphere and experience colorful learning environment. In addition, I am well prepared linguistically to further my studies in the U.S.A. My IELTS is 8.5 and my GRE is 160. I am cheerful, lively, outgoing and have a strong ability to adapt to a new environment. During my after-school time, with a strong sense of responsibility and good team spirit, I have always actively involved in community activities and worked in the student community. Movies, basketball, football and other sports are my favorites in my spare time. After hardworking of a couple of years, and I achieved a lot. The availability of going to Michigan State University for exchange is very important for me, I sincerely hope that I can get this opportunity. As one of the world's leading research universities, to study at Michigan State University was my dream from my childhood, and will fulfill my great desire. What's more, the university's values and the principles of academic freedom allow faculty members at the university to pursue their educational and research interests without interference, and this atmosphere matches my personality well.

I understand that the exchange program of physics at the State University of Michigan enjoys a worldwide reputation and that the faculty in the field of urban design is especially strong. The fine academic atmosphere and the first-class teaching and research will keep me up to date with the world's cutting edge developments of architecture. Furthermore, its location in Michigan will provide me with a unique perspective on the challenges facing

American science education in the 21st.

With a solid academic background and practical experience in the field, I believe the proposed exchange program will provide me with a broader view and exceptional creativity in seeking effective solutions to the related problems in science education in contemporary China.

To be more competitive in such a multi-dimensional field as an educational researcher, I believe my propose exchange program is of great importance to my future professional growth and success. With my deep-rooted interest in education and the recognition of the quality of your university program, I hope you will give my application every consideration.

Useful Expressions

1. Family influence

(1) Under the influence of my father, I aspired to practice medicine.

(2) I am so grateful that I was born in a happy family, in an artistic atmosphere, and fortunately, owing to encouragement from my parents, I was able to develop my interests and strived for a career in art.

(3) As a child, I often accompanied my father to his small coin shop and spent hours watching him work. This experience instilled in me the desire to own and manage my own business someday.

(4) As my parents are professors, I started reading edifying books very early in my life, which gradually fostered my sound personalities.

2. Your interest

(1) Having majored in world literature as an undergraduate, I would like to concentrate on English and American literature.

(2) My interest in social science dates back to my years in college, where I had the opportunity to study a number of subjects in the humanities and they have been both enjoyable and enlightening, providing me with a new and different perspective on the world in which we live.

(3) I am especially interested in the information technology industry.

(4) Computing science and its applications have always fascinated me and for the reason, I have found my A-level courses extremely interesting.

(5) To make myself more insightful, I need training in a broader theoretical framework. That is why I am now eager to pursue further study in your program.

(6) When I began my undergraduate career, I had the opportunity to be exposed to the full range of engineering courses, all of which tended to reinforce and solidify my intense interest in engineering.

3. Objectives/Career goals

(1) My sincerest desire is to become a computer scientist. Specifically, I am interested in exploring how problems can be modeled and solved using artificial intelligence. I also want to learn about human cognition and machine intelligence.

(2) I wish to further my study in the field of American literature, working toward a master's degree at first, and then, if possible, toward a doctoral degree.

(3) Much of what I've encountered might easily have dissuaded me from seeking a career in law, but instead, I find that I am more eager than ever to prepare myself to become a lawyer.

(4) In terms of career, I see myself teaching literature, writing criticism and editing or publishing poetry.

(5) Upon completing my academic goals, I shall return to continue my research in this field.

(6) For the next three years, I hope to join a program that will impart a solid foundation in the science and technical practice of medicine, while maintaining a personal connection with the patients. Eventually, I aspire to a career in academic medicine, which will allow me to increase my effectiveness as an educator and researcher.

4. Education

(1) I achieved a score of GPA 3.8, the highest among the 80 students in my grade.

(2) In the four years' study at Shandong University, I studied strenuously and was awarded a prize which only students in the top five percent could obtain; I performed successfully in all the major courses with a GPA of 3.8.

(3) One year ago, I earned my undergraduate degree in mechanical engineering at Southwest University.

(4) In recognition of my outstanding record, I was selected to do a graduate program, exempt from the mandatory entrance examination, a privilege given only to a few of the best students each year.

(5) I was admitted to the graduate program at the Department of Management to further my studies, and I attained my master's degree in 2005.

5. Academic/Research experience

(1) In Fudan University, I completed not only the program of mechanical and electronic engineering but also all the core courses of telecommunication engineering.

(2) As a mathematics major, I have developed the analytical proficiency that is necessary for working through complex problems. My courses in statistics have especially prepared me for data analysis, and my more theoretical courses have taught me how to construct an effective argument.

(3) By majoring in electrical engineering with a concentration on biomedical engineering, I have exposed to all facets of scientific and analytical disciplines, from mathematics to circuit analysis.

(4) I was chosen in June 2003 to work as a student research assistant to Prof. Lin Yuan at the Institute of China's Economy, Xiamen University.

(5) My recent work includes several articles dealing in various ways with consciousness in fiction: I am becoming increasingly interested in the idea of fictional "character" and in characterization. I should also admit to writing fiction of my own. My novel Aristotle Detective, first published in 1978, was translated into Italian in late 1999, and the event resurrected my fiction-writing career. It was such a "hit" in Italy that the publisher Sellerio then published it in booklet form.

6. Personal Ability/attribute

(1) I can definitely assure you of my intelligence, diligence and good performance in all the courses required.

(2) I wish to assure you that I have the necessary English skills to complete advanced studies and research in your PH.D. program. I passed CET-6 and got a score of 7.0 in IELTS, and I have been reading academic or professional materials in English widely.

My strengths include the ability to network effectively within the business and social community, expertise in the consultative sales process, and understanding of nonprofit and volunteer management.

(3) My life to date has prepared me to deal with many obstacles and also has shown me the determination, strength, and caring that are a part of my character. As I look forward to my future in medicine, I believe these characteristics will enable me to succeed and be a valuable asset to the profession.

(4) In addition to becoming more aware of both the judicial process and people in general, I have also become more compassionate, more patient, and more diplomatic as a result of my time at the superior court.

7. Hobbies and activities

(1) My other interests include music and sports, such as football, tennis and general fitness. Ever since a freshman, I have been a member of the college football team.

(2) Besides studying hard for my courses, I like to read extensively in related fields, such as science fiction and physics.

(3) Through campus organizations and volunteer work, I have also made an effort to contribute both to the university and to the surrounding community.

(4) Apart from my studies, I have also paid attention to enhancing my working and communication skills. I was the chief editor of the magazine run by the university's English society.

参考文献

[1] GASTEL B, DAY A R. How to write and publish a scientific paper[M]. Beijing: Publishing House of Electronics Industry, 2018.

[2] DAVIS L B, 王梅英. 研究生英语科技论文写作[M]. 北京：高等教育出版社，2006.

[3] COYKE W, LAW J. Research papers[M]. Beijing: Beijing Language and Culture University Press, 2019.

[4] WALLACE S. 参加国际学术会议必须要做的那些事：给华人作者的特别忠告[M]. 北京：北京大学出版社，2015.

[5] 丁往道，吴冰，钟美荪，等. 英语写作手册[M]. 北京：外语教学与研究出版社，2008.

[6] 王景惠. 新科学家英语：硕博英语演讲与写作[M]. 哈尔滨：哈尔滨工业大学出版，2002.

[7] 王慧莉，贾卫国. 国际学术交流英语[M]. 大连：大连理工大学出版社，2005.

[8] 张俊东. SCI论文写作和发表: You Can Do It [M]. 北京：化学工业出版社，2016.

[9] 董绣. 国际会议交流英语[M]. 上海：同济大学出版社，2011.

[10] 郭继荣，刘新法. 学术交流英语[M]. 西安：西安交通大学出版社，2008.

[11] 洪卫. 学术交际英语[M]. 北京：电子工业出版社，2012.

[12] 胡庚申. 英语论文写作与发表[M]. 北京：高等教育出版社，2000.

[13] 胡庚申. 国际会议交流英语[M]. 北京：高等教育出版社，2007.

[14] 贾卫国. 国际学术交流英语[M]. 北京：外语教学与研究出版社，2008.

[15] 姜怡，姜欣. 学术交流英语[M]. 北京：高等教育出版社，2006.

[16] 唐国全. 科技英语论文报告写作[M]. 北京：北京航天航空大学出版社，2004.

[17] 朱月珍. 英语科技学术论文[M]. 武昌：华中科技大学出版社，2006.